# AQA STUDY GUIDE

# GCSE 9–1
# MACBETH

BY WILLIAM SHAKESPEARE

REVISION &
PRACTICE
ALL IN ONE BOOK

**Author** Richard Durant

**Series Consultants** Richard Durant and Cindy Torn

**Reviewer** Rob Pollard

**Editorial team** Rachel Morgan, Audrey Stokes, Camilla Erskine, Lesley Densham, Mary Colson, Louise Titley

**Typesetting** Oxford Designers and Illustrators

**Cover design** Neil Salt and Nicolle Thomas

**App development** Hannah Barnett, Phil Crothers and Haremi Ltd

**Acknowledgements**

**Illustration** Paul Crompton/Oxford Designers & Illustrators

**Photographs** pages 13 and 72: lightning, DR-images/Shutterstock; page 16: crow with crown, tomertu/Shutterstock; page 24: diamond, La Gorda/Shutterstock; pages 24 and 30: dagger, burnel1/Shutterstock; page 26: castle gate, Blazar SLU/Shutterstock; pages 26, 36, 46 and 72: blood splatters, MrsPopman1985/Shutterstock; page 34: scorpion silhouette, Algonga/Shutterstock; page 34 and 80: stars, Zacarias Pereira da Mata/Shutterstock; page 40: crow, Jennifer Uppendahl/Shutterstock; page 44: tree, Banana Republic images/Shutterstock; pages 56 and 79: candle, mrkornflakes/Shutterstock; page 62: cross, Lunatictm/Shutterstock; page 70: King James I, The Print Collector/Alamy Stock Photo; page 74: scorpion, sunstock/iStock; page 76: royal orb, Evgeny freeone/Shutterstock; page 81: tragedy mask, A.B.G./Shutterstock; page 84: girl doing exam, Monkey Business Images/Shutterstock; page 91: notepad and pen, TRINACRIA PHOTO/Shutterstock

Designed using Adobe InDesign

Published by Scholastic Education, an imprint of Scholastic Ltd, Book End, Range Road, Witney, Oxfordshire, OX29 0YD
Registered office: Westfield Road, Southam, Warwickshire CV47 0RA
www.scholastic.co.uk

Printed by Bell and Bain
© 2019 Scholastic Ltd
1 2 3 4 5 6 7 8 9  9 0 1 2 3 4 5 6 7 8

**British Library Cataloguing-in-Publication Data**
A catalogue record for this book is available from the British Library.

ISBN 978-1407-18260-5

**Note from the publisher:**
Please use this product in conjunction with the official specification and sample assessment materials. Ask your teacher if you are unsure where to find them.

# Contents

**Check your answers on the free revision app or at www.scholastic.co.uk/gcse**

# How to use this book

This Study Guide is designed to help you prepare effectively for your AQA GCSE English literature exam question on *Macbeth* (Paper 1, Section A).

The content has been organised in a sequence that builds confidence, and which will deepen your knowledge and understanding of the play step by step. Therefore, it is best to work through this book in the order that it is presented.

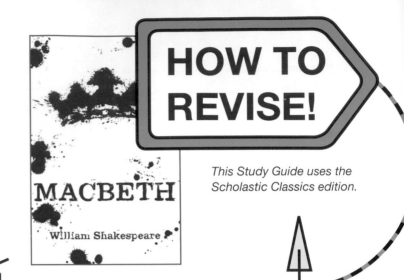

**HOW TO REVISE!**

*This Study Guide uses the Scholastic Classics edition.*

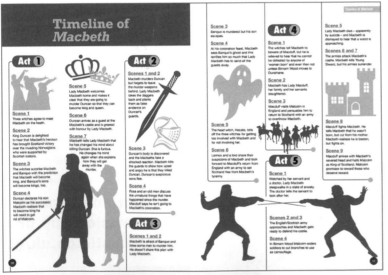

## Know the plot

**1** It is very important that you know the plot well: to be clear about what happens and in what order. The **timeline** on pages 10–11 provides a useful overview of the plot, highlighting key events.

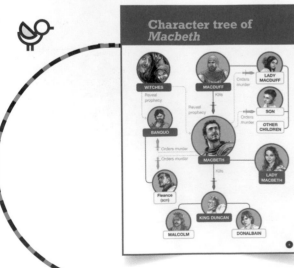

The **character tree** on page 9 introduces you to the main characters of the text.

# The chronological section

**2** The **chronological section** on pages 12–63 takes you through the play scene by scene, providing plot summaries and pointing out important details. It is also designed to help you think about the structure of the play.

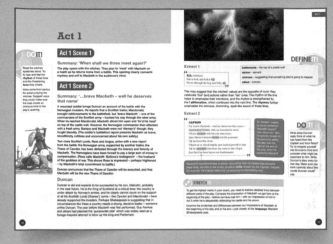

This section provides an in-depth exploration of themes or character development, drawing your attention to how Shakespeare's language choices reveal the play's meaning.

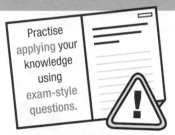

Practise applying your knowledge using exam-style questions.

# The play as a whole

**3** The second half of the guide is retrospective: it helps you to look back over the whole play through a number of relevant 'lenses': characters, themes, Shakespeare's language, verse forms and structural features

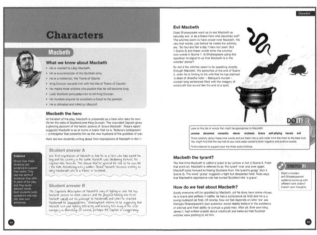

# Doing well in your AQA Exam

Stick to the **TIME LIMITS** you will need to in the exam.

**4** Finally, you will find an extended 'Doing well in your AQA exam' section which guides you through the process of understanding questions, and planning and writing answers.

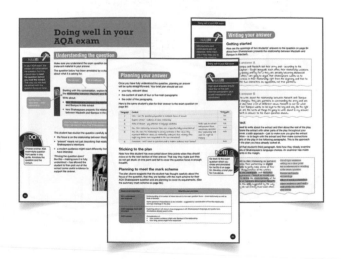

# Features of this guide

The best way to retain information is to take an active approach to revision.

Throughout this book, you will find lots of features that will make your revision an active, successful process.

## SNAPIT!

Use the Snap it! feature in the revision app to take pictures of key concepts and information. Great for revision on the go!

### DEFINEIT!

Explains the meaning of difficult words from the set texts.

**Callouts** Additional explanations of important points.

words shown in **purple bold** can be found in the glossary on pages 94–95

Find methods of relaxation that work for you throughout the revision period.

Regular exercise helps stimulate the brain and will help you relax.

### DOIT!

Activities to embed your knowledge and understanding and prepare you for the exams.

### NAILIT!

Succinct and vital tips on how to do well in your exam.

### STRETCHIT!

Provides content that stretches you further.

### REVIEW IT!

Helps you to consolidate and understand what you have learned before moving on.

Revise in pairs or small groups and deliver presentations on topics to each other.

### AQA exam-style question

AQA exam-style sample questions based on the extract shown are given on some pages. Use the sample mark scheme on page 86 to help you assess your responses. This will also help you understand what you could do to improve your response.

FOR HIGH-MARK QUESTIONS, SPEND TIME **PLANNING** YOUR ANSWER!

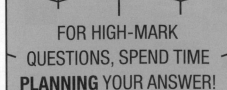

# FREE REVISION APP

- The **free revision app** can be downloaded to your mobile phone (iOS and Android), making **on-the-go revision** easy.

- Use the revision calendar to help map out your revision in the lead-up to the exam.

- Complete multiple-choice questions and create your own SNAP**IT!** revision cards.

**www.scholastic.co.uk/gcse**

## Online answers and additional resources

All of the tasks in this book are designed to get you thinking and to consolidate your understanding through thought and application. Therefore, it is important to write your own answers before checking. Some questions include tables where you need to fill in your answer in the book. Other questions require you to use a separate piece of paper so that you can draft your response and work out the best way of answering.

Make notes on different aspects of the relationship between Macbeth and Lady Macbeth. Look at how they communicate and try to influence each other. Complete the table for other parts of the play.

| Scene | Relationship between Macbeth and Lady Macbeth |
|---|---|
| Act 1, Scene 5 | Macbeth is reunited with his wife on returning home from war. She calls him 'great' perhaps to flatter him and make him easier to manipulate. He calls her 'dearest love' which probably expresses genuine love, making him more open to manipulation. |

Get plenty of sleep, especially the night before an exam.

**LOOK AFTER YOURSELF**

Help your brain by looking after your whole body!

Once you have worked through a section, you can check your answers to Do it!, Stretch it!, Review it! and the exam practice sections on the app or at **www.scholastic.co.uk/gcse**.

# An introduction to your AQA Shakespeare text

## Why study *Macbeth*?

Although *Macbeth* was written more than 400 years ago, it has kept its appeal for modern audiences. The subject matter of the play still has a strong relevance. A powerful military man assassinates his country's leader in order to gain total power for himself. To hang on to power he recruits a shadowy band of spies and assassins to terrify the population into obeying him. Over the last fifty years many countries have been ruled in roughly this way.

The tyrant-rulers of those countries are nearly always men, but they are often supported by women whose frustration at being excluded from power forces them to pursue their own ambitions through their husband.

The plot of *Macbeth* charts all these issues: power, ambition, the conflict between good and evil, and the unequal relationship between men and women.

## *Macbeth* in your AQA exam

*Macbeth* is examined in Section A (the first half) of the first AQA GCSE English Literature exam, Paper 1 Shakespeare and the 19th-century novel. Here is how it fits into the overall assessment framework:

| Paper 1     Time: **1 hour 45 minutes** | Paper 2     Time: **2 hours 15 minutes** |
| --- | --- |
| **Section A: Shakespeare: *Macbeth*** | Section A: Modern prose or drama |
| Section B: 19th-century novel | Section B: Poetry anthology |
| | Section C: Unseen poetry |

There will be just one question on *Macbeth* and you should not answer questions on any other Shakespeare play. Just answer the *Macbeth* question. You should spend 55 minutes planning and writing your answer to the question. There are 30 marks available for the Shakespeare question, plus four extra marks for good vocabulary, spelling, sentences and punctuation (VSSP, sometimes called 'SPaG').

The Shakespeare question will come with a short extract from the play printed on your exam paper. You will find the question straight after the extract. The question will focus on character and/or theme. You must answer the question in relation to the extract and to other relevant parts of the play that you have chosen.

## A character tree

The 'character tree' on page 9 should help you to fix in your mind the names of the characters, their relationships and who did what to whom.

## Timeline of *Macbeth*

The timeline of pages 10–11 provides a visual overview of the plot, highlighting key events which take place over the course of the play. It will also help you to think about the structure of the play.

# Character tree of *Macbeth*

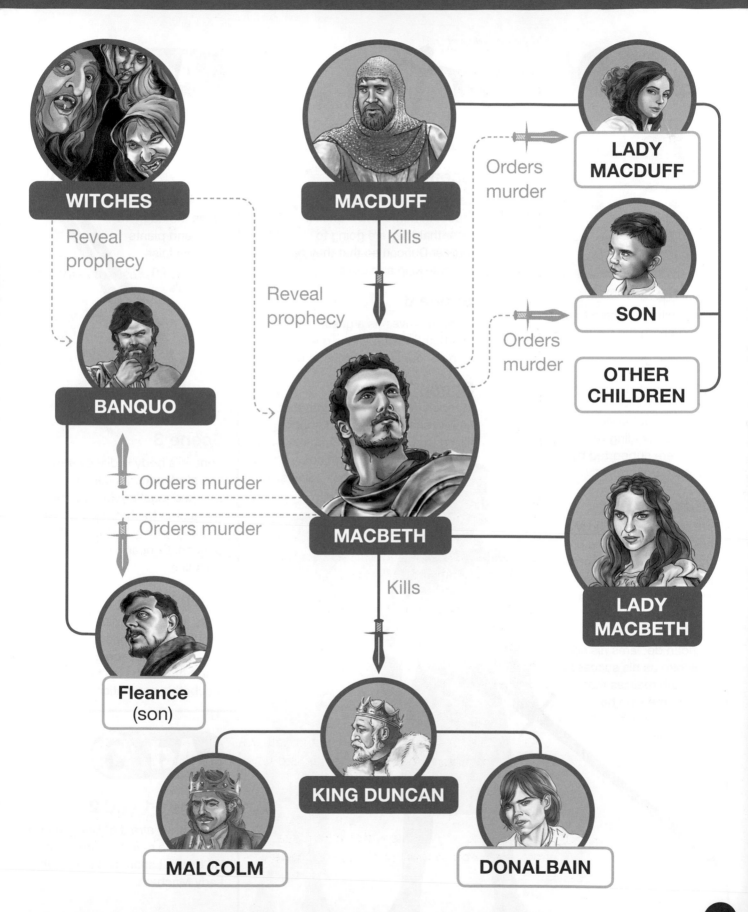

WITCHES

MACDUFF

LADY MACDUFF

Orders murder

Reveal prophecy

Kills

Reveal prophecy

SON

Orders murder

OTHER CHILDREN

BANQUO

MACBETH

Orders murder

Orders murder

LADY MACBETH

Kills

Fleance (son)

KING DUNCAN

MALCOLM

DONALBAIN

# Timeline of Macbeth

## Act 1

### Scene 1

Three witches agree to meet Macbeth on the heath.

### Scene 2

King Duncan is delighted to hear that Macbeth's heroism has brought Scotland victory over the invading Norwegians who were supported by Scottish traitors.

### Scene 3

The witches surprise Macbeth and Banquo with the prediction that Macbeth will become king, and Banquo's sons will become kings, too.

### Scene 4

Duncan declares his son Malcolm as his successor. Macbeth realises that to become king he will need to get rid of Malcolm.

### Scene 5

Lady Macbeth welcomes Macbeth home and makes it clear that they are going to murder Duncan so that they can become king and queen.

### Scene 6

Duncan arrives as a guest at the Macbeth's castle and is greeted with honour by Lady Macbeth.

### Scene 7

Macbeth tells Lady Macbeth that he has changed his mind about killing Duncan. She is furious. He changes his mind again when she explains how they will get away with the murder.

## Act 2

### Scenes 1 and 2

Macbeth murders Duncan but forgets to leave the murder weapons behind. Lady Macbeth takes the daggers back and plants them as false evidence on Duncan's guards.

### Scene 3

Duncan's body is discovered and the Macbeths fake a shocked reaction. Macbeth kills the guards to show how upset and angry he is that they killed Duncan. Duncan's suspicious sons flee.

### Scene 4

Ross and an old man discuss the unnatural things that have happened since the murder. Macduff says he isn't going to Macbeth's coronation.

## Act 3

### Scenes 1 and 2

Macbeth is afraid of Banquo and hires some men to murder him. He doesn't share this plan with Lady Macbeth.

## Scene 3

Banquo is murdered but his son escapes.

## Scene 4

At his coronation feast, Macbeth sees Banquo's ghost and this terrifies him so much that Lady Macbeth has to send all the guests away.

## Scene 5

The head witch, Hecate, tells off the three witches for getting too involved with Macbeth and for not involving her.

## Scene 6

Lennox and a lord share their suspicions of Macbeth and look forward to Macduff's return from England with an army to set Scotland free from Macbeth's tyranny.

## Act 4

## Scene 1

The witches tell Macbeth to beware of Macduff, but he is relieved to hear that he cannot be defeated by anyone of 'woman born' and even then not unless Birnam Wood moves to Dunsinane.

## Scene 2

Macbeth has Lady Macduff, her family and her servants slaughtered.

## Scene 3

Macduff visits Malcolm in England and persuades him to return to Scotland with an army to overthrow Macbeth.

## Act 5

## Scene 1

Watched by her servant and a doctor, Lady Macbeth sleepwalks in a state of anxiety. The doctor tells the servant to look after her.

## Scenes 2 and 3

The English/Scottish army approaches and Macbeth gets ready to defend his castle.

## Scene 4

In Birnam Wood Malcolm orders soldiers to cut branches to use as camouflage.

## Scene 5

Lady Macbeth dies – apparently by suicide – and Macbeth is dismayed to hear that a wood is approaching.

## Scenes 6 and 7

The armies attack Macbeth's castle. Macbeth kills Young Siward, but his armies surrender.

## Scene 8

Macduff fights Macbeth. He tells Macbeth that he wasn't born, but cut from his mother. Macbeth realises he is beaten, but fights on.

## Scene 9

Macduff arrives with Macbeth's severed head and hails Malcolm as King of Scotland. Malcolm promises to reward those who deserve reward.

# Act 1

## DO IT!

Read the witches' speeches aloud. Try to hear and feel the **rhythm** of these lines and the threatening **tone** they create.

Write some brief advice for actors playing the witches. Suggest ways they could make sure the lines create an ominous tone to the play's opening.

## Act 1 Scene 1

### Summary: 'When shall we three meet again?'

The play opens with the witches. They plan to 'meet' with Macbeth on a heath as he returns home from a battle. This opening clearly connects mystery and evil to Macbeth in the audience's mind.

## Act 1 Scene 2

### Summary: '…brave Macbeth – well he deserves that name'

A wounded soldier brings Duncan an account of the battle with the Norwegian invaders. He reports that a Scottish traitor, Macdonald, brought reinforcements to the battlefield, but 'brave Macbeth' – one of the commanders of the Scottish army – hacked his way through the rebel army. When he reached Macdonald, Macbeth sliced him open and 'fix'd his head' on top of the castle wall. However, the Norwegian commander then attacked with a fresh army. Banquo and Macbeth were not 'dismay'd' though: they fought bloodily. (The soldier's battlefront report presents Macbeth as brave, bloodthirsty, ruthless and unconcerned about his own safety.)

Two more Scottish Lords, Ross and Angus, arrive with a new report from the battle: the Norwegian army, supported by another traitor, the Thane of Cawdor, has been defeated through the bravery and ferocity of Macbeth. The Norwegians have been forced to pay a large sum of money in compensation. (Ross calls Macbeth 'Bellona's bridegroom' – the husband of the goddess of war. This shows Ross is impressed – perhaps frightened – by Macbeth's total commitment to battle.)

Duncan announces that the Thane of Cawdor will be executed, and that Macbeth will be the new Thane of Cawdor.

## Duncan

Duncan is old and expects to be succeeded by his son, Malcolm, probably in the near future. He is the King of Scotland at a critical time: the country is under attack by Norway's armies, and he clearly cannot count on the support of all his Scottish Lords ('thanes'): some – like Cawdor and Macdonald – have already supported the invaders. Perhaps Shakespeare is suggesting that in circumstances like these a country needs a strong, decisive leader – someone *un*like Duncan. The year before *Macbeth* was first performed, Guy Fawkes and others had planned the 'gunpowder plot' which was widely seen as a foreign-inspired attempt to blow up the king and Parliament.

## Extract 1

**DEFINE IT!**

> **ALL** (witches)
> Fair is foul, and foul is fair.
> Hover through the fog and filthy air.

**battlements** – the top of a castle wall

**minion** – servant

**ominous** – suggesting that something bad is going to happen

**valour** – bravery

This may suggest that the witches' values are the opposite of ours: they celebrate 'foul' (evil) actions rather than 'fair' ones. The rhythm of the line helps to emphasise their intentions, and the rhythm is strengthened by the f **alliteration**, which continues into the next line. The **rhymes** further emphasise the ominous, drumming, spell-like sound of these lines.

## Extract 2

> **CAPTAIN**
> For brave Macbeth – well he deserves that name –
> Disdaining Fortune, with his brandish'd steel,
> Which smoked with bloody execution,
> Like Valour's minion carved out his passage
> 5 Till he faced the slave,
> Which ne'er shook hands, nor bade farewell to him,
> Till he unseam'd him from the nave to the chaps,
> And fix'd his head upon our battlements.

To 'disdain' means to show contempt: Macbeth doesn't care about his 'fate': he ignores threats to his personal safety. We also see this right at the end of the play when he confronts Macduff.

Macbeth's bloodthirstiness is shown not just by how he treated Macdonald's dead body, but also in the brutal, physical **verbs** chosen by the Captain. Despite his wounds, the Captain seems to be enjoying his storytelling role!

**DO IT!**

What does Duncan really think of what he has heard from the Captain and from Ross? Try to imagine yourself into Duncan's mind and consider what might be important to him. Write Duncan's diary entry for that day. Make sure you think carefully about the words Duncan would use.

## STRETCH IT!

To get the highest marks in your exam, you need to explore detailed links between different parts of the play. Compare the impression of Macbeth we get here at the beginning of the play – before we have met him – with our impression of him in Act 5 when he is desperately defending his castle and his crown.

Examine the similarities and differences between our impressions of Macbeth at the beginning of the play and at the end. Look closely at the **language** Macbeth (Shakespeare) uses.

## Act 1 Scene 3

### Summary: 'All hail, Macbeth, that shalt be King'

The witches meet on the heath and share stories of how they have tormented humans. (Note the hypnotic **effect** of the witches' short, rhyming lines. In the lines 'A drum, a drum!/Macbeth doth come' we can almost hear an ominous drum beat.)

Macbeth and Banquo arrive and wonder if the witches are women or 'fantastical' beings. They astonish Macbeth by greeting him as Thane of Cawdor and telling him he will be king. The witches tell Banquo that his sons will become kings. Macbeth demands that the witches explain their predictions but they vanish, leaving Banquo and Macbeth to wonder if they have imagined them. (Macbeth and Banquo seem to react differently to the witches. Perhaps Banquo does not take the witches seriously, while Macbeth seems to be completely taken over ('rapt') by their predictions.)

When Ross and Angus arrive, they inform Macbeth that he is Thane of Cawdor now that the previous thane is to be executed. Banquo warns Macbeth that the devil can work this way – telling someone a surprising truth in order to lure them into an evil act.

While Banquo talks to Ross and Angus, Macbeth tries to make sense of his reactions to the witches' predictions and how they have been supported by Ross's news. He is terrified by the thoughts of murder that enter his imagination, but he decides that perhaps he will simply become king without having to take any action at all. (Note that the idea of murder as a way of becoming king already occurs to Macbeth here. He does hope he can become king 'Without my stir', so perhaps he expects Duncan to make him his heir.)

Macbeth quietly tells Banquo that he wants to talk to him later about their strange experience on the heath, and about what it might mean.

### The supernatural

The witches seem to control Macbeth. Just before Macbeth enters, the witches say, 'Peace! The charm's wound up', as though they have cast a hypnotic spell over him, taking control of him. His first words echo the witches' earlier words, as though they have put the words into his mouth: 'So foul and fair a day I have not seen'.

**DO IT!**

Here are eight words that *might* describe Macbeth's reaction to the witches:

surprised

excited

terrified

contemptuous

worried

angry

pleased

spell-bound

Choose the two words which you consider to be *most* true about Macbeth's reaction. Briefly explain your choices.

## Extract 1

Macbeth is used to getting his way through force, but this has no effect on the witches: they are beyond his control.

> **BANQUO**
> If you can look into the seeds of time,
> And say which grain will grow and which will not,
> Speak then to me, who neither beg nor fear
> Your favours nor your hate.
> **FIRST WITCH**
> 5 Hail!
> **SECOND WITCH**
> Hail!
> **THIRD WITCH**
> Hail!
> **FIRST WITCH**
> Lesser than Macbeth, and greater.
> **SECOND WITCH**
> Not so happy, yet much happier.
> **THIRD WITCH**
> 10 Thou shalt get kings, though thou be none.
> So all hail, Macbeth and Banquo!
> **FIRST WITCH**
> Banquo and Macbeth, all hail!
> **MACBETH**
> Stay, you imperfect speakers, tell me more.
> By Sinel's death, I know I am Thane of Glamis;
> 15 But how of Cawdor? The Thane of Cawdor lives,
> A prosperous gentleman; and to be King
> Stands not within the prospect of belief,
> No more than to be Cawdor. Say from whence
> You owe this strange intelligence, or why
> 20 Upon this blasted heath you stop our way
> With such prophetic greeting? Speak, I charge you.

**Banquo seems to have a sort of 'take it or leave it' reaction to the witches. He makes out that he doesn't fear them or particularly care about what they say.**

**Here, instead of repeating each other's words, the witches repeat each other's sentence structures and riddling style. The effect is hypnotic.**

**Here the First Witch repeats the Third Witch's words, just altering the order.**

**Macbeth's response to the witches is commanding, and that is shown in his repeated use of imperative verbs.**

**The witches always 'mirror' each other's words. This emphasises their unity.**

## DEFINE IT!

**Sinel** – Macbeth's father; Macbeth is swearing on his own father to convey his seriousness

**get** – have children

**prophetic** – telling the future; predicting

**prosperous** – well off; wealthy; happy

**supernatural** – something that is beyond the control of natural forces; magical

**thou** - you

## DO IT!

Make a note of points in the play where supernatural forces seem to be particularly significant.

### AQA exam-style question

Starting with this conversation, explore how Shakespeare presents the influence of the supernatural in *Macbeth*.

Write about:

- how Shakespeare presents the influence of the supernatural in this conversation

- how Shakespeare presents the influence of the supernatural in the play as a whole.

[30 marks]

Use the guidance on pages 84–87 to help you plan your answer.

# Act 1 Scene 4

## Summary: 'Let not light see my black and deep desires'

Malcolm reports to Duncan that Cawdor faced his execution bravely. Duncan is amazed that a person's face can give no indication of their true thoughts: he had 'an absolute trust' in Cawdor. (Does this suggest Duncan is a poor judge of character?)

Macbeth and Banquo arrive. Duncan cannot thank them enough, but they both say that serving Duncan is enough reward in itself.

Duncan makes his oldest son, Malcolm, heir to the throne. Macbeth has 'black and deep desires' to kill Malcolm to get the crown for himself. (Macbeth's use of the word 'black' links his murderous intentions to darkness and night, the perfect cover for his plans.)

Duncan tells Macbeth he will come to stay with him that night. Macbeth says his wife will be 'joyful' to hear of this honour. (Duncan trusts Macbeth, calling him 'a peerless kinsman'.)

 **STRETCH**IT!

If Macbeth was willing to risk his own life in battle to save Scotland and its king, why does he now consider killing the very man he was – in effect – protecting? Does Macbeth blame Duncan's trust for traitors like Cawdor for putting his own life and Scotland's independence in peril? Perhaps Shakespeare is suggesting the war has proved that Scotland needs Macbeth, not Duncan.

## Act 1 Scene 5

### Summary: 'Leave all the rest to me'

Lady Macbeth reads Macbeth's letter, summarising what has happened. She is excited about becoming queen but fears Macbeth is not ruthless enough to kill Duncan. (In Lady Macbeth's experience, Macbeth insists on achieving ambitions 'holily' – killing only in warfare.)

Hearing that Duncan will be staying the night, she calls on spirits to fill her with 'direst cruelty' so that she can kill Duncan. (By having Lady Macbeth call on 'spirits', Shakespeare makes her sound like a witch.)

Macbeth arrives and she tells him she is excited about their futures. She insists that Duncan will die before morning. Macbeth only has to keep an innocent face and 'leave all the rest' to her.

## DO IT!

Write some notes on how these two scenes suggest appearances cannot always be trusted.

Base your notes on at least two short quotations.

17

## Extract 1

Lady Macbeth's words in this speech are violent and shocking.

Lady Macbeth repeats the imperative verb, 'come'. This repetition makes her sound determined and commanding.

Notice how Shakespeare sometimes uses very direct, shocking language and images when he wants to show Lady Macbeth's determination and lack of 'squeamishness'.

"

**LADY MACBETH**

Come, you spirits
That tend on mortal thoughts, unsex me here
And fill me from the crown to the toe top – full
Of direst cruelty! Make thick my blood,
5 Stop up the access and passage to remorse,
That no compunctious visitings of nature
Shake my fell purpose nor keep peace between
The effect and it! Come to my woman's breasts,
And take my milk for gall, your murdering ministers,
10 Wherever in your sightless substances
You wait on nature's mischief! Come, thick night,
And pall thee in the dunnest smoke of hell
That my keen knife see not the wound it makes,
Nor heaven peep through the blanket of the dark
15 To cry, "Hold, hold."

"

'Unsex' is Lady Macbeth's request for her conventional female gentleness to be replaced with tougher, traditionally male tendencies.

Lady Macbeth welcomes the powers of evil and darkness to help her achieve her ambition. Her many monosyllabic words give her speech a 'punchy' directness and brutality, emphasising her decisiveness.

## Lady Macbeth compared with Macbeth

Lady Macbeth realises the danger of delay and indecision. Macbeth, too, realises 'Words to the heat of deeds too cold breath gives.' (Act 2 Scene 1). Like her husband, Lady Macbeth cannot bear the thought of *seeing* her crimes.

**DEFINE IT!**

**compunctious** – guilt-creating

**dunnest** – darkest, thickest

**fell** – fierce, violent

**fiend** – evil spirit, devil, wicked person

**pall** – cover in a burial gown

**remorse** – sorrow, regret, guilt

**sightless substances** – invisible spirits

**squeamish** – unable to bear unpleasant sights or feelings

### AQA exam-style question

At the end of the play, the new King Malcolm calls Lady Macbeth 'fiend-like'.

Starting with this speech, explore how far you agree with this opinion.

Write about:

- how far Shakespeare presents Lady Macbeth as 'fiend-like' in this speech

- how far Shakespeare presents Lady Macbeth as 'fiend-like' in the play as a whole.

[30 marks]

Use the guidance on pages 84–87 to help you plan your answer.

## Act 1 Scene 6

### Summary: 'See, see, our honour'd hostess!'

Duncan, his sons and lords arrive at Macbeth's castle. They are all impressed by the atmosphere of peace and gentleness. They sense 'heaven's breath' in the building. (There is **dramatic irony** here: Duncan feels entirely safe just at the moment we know he is in danger.)

Lady Macbeth receives Duncan. They exchange enthusiastic praises and Lady Macbeth promises that serving Duncan is a deep pleasure for her. (Lady Macbeth is highly skilled at following her own advice, 'look like the innocent flower,/But be the serpent under it' (Act 1 Scene 5) and showing a false face.)

## Act 1 Scene 7

### Summary: 'Bring forth men-children only'

Macbeth worries about the consequences of killing Duncan. It would be wrong to kill a man who is his king and his guest. Duncan has been such a good and gentle king that Macbeth fears 'damnation' for his murder. He also fears that his huge ambition will cause his own downfall.

Lady Macbeth is appalled by Macbeth's change of mind and accuses him of cowardice, unmanliness, not loving her, and failure to keep a promise.

Her plan to murder Duncan and have the blame put on the guards so impresses Macbeth that he decides to go ahead with the murder after all. (Did Shakespeare want us to blame Lady Macbeth for turning Macbeth into a murderer? Certainly Macbeth has a conscience and is reluctant to kill Duncan, but look carefully at what finally persuades him to go ahead with the murder: *he believes he won't be caught.* This suggests his objection to murder was not really a *moral* objection: it was a *practical* one.)

### Why Macbeth kills Duncan

Here is part of what a student wrote about why Macbeth decides to kill Duncan. Note how the student supports points with evidence. An examiner's notes are next to the student's answer.

| | |
|---|---|
| When the witches told Macbeth he would be king, he almost immediately imagined murder as a way of becoming king. He thought that before he had spoken to his wife, so she didn't plant the idea in his head. She just came up with the perfect plan. | Good use of indirect evidence – reference to detail earlier in play. |
| | Clear, well-argued point, backed with more indirect evidence. 'So' used to signal step in the argument. |

**DO IT!**

Write down all the reasons Shakespeare suggests for why Macbeth decides to kill Duncan.

You could use these reasons to develop the student's response.

# DEFINE IT!

**corporal** – of the body

**feat** – achievement

**mettle** – courage, strength of spirit

**quell** – slaughter, crush

**spongy** – drunk; (they have soaked up alcohol)

**thy** - your

**undaunted** – never put off or discouraged

Lady Macbeth is still careful: she continues to use rhetorical questions to gently secure Macbeth's agreement, without triggering his objections again.

## Extract 1

" - - - - - - - - - - - - - - - - - - - - - - - - - - - - - - - - - - -

**LADY MACBETH**

What cannot you and I perform upon
The unguarded Duncan? What not put upon
His spongy officers, who shall bear the guilt
Of our great quell?

**MACBETH**

5 Bring forth men-children only,
For thy undaunted mettle should compose
Nothing but males. Will it not be received,
When we have mark'd with blood those sleepy two
Of his own chamber, and us'd their very daggers,
10 That they have done't?

**LADY MACBETH**

Who dares receive it other,
As we shall make our griefs and clamour roar
Upon his death?

**MACBETH**

I am settled and bend up
15 Each corporal agent to this terrible feat.
Away, and mock the time with fairest show
False face must hide what the false heart doth know.

- - - - - - - - - - - - - - - - - - - - - - - - - - - - - - - - - - - "

Lady Macbeth uses **rhetorical questions** to persuade her husband. It is as though she is slipping ideas into his head, getting round his objections gently.

Note that Macbeth changes his attitude because *they will get away with* the murder, not because it is a right thing to do. Macbeth thinks that his wife's ruthlessness and courage are manly characteristics. Is he impressed or appalled with her 'manliness'?

These lines end the scene. Typically Shakespeare uses a **rhyming couplet** to round off the scene neatly, and also to emphasise the **proverb**-like last line. Pretence and being deceptive is crucial to their plan.

Now Macbeth is speaking decisively and assertively – as though he has come up with the plan!

## AQA exam-style question

Starting with this conversation, explore how Shakespeare presents the relationship between Macbeth and Lady Macbeth in *Macbeth*.

Write about:

- how Shakespeare presents the relationship between Macbeth and Lady Macbeth in this conversation

- how Shakespeare presents the relationship between Macbeth and Lady Macbeth in the play as a whole.

[30 marks]

Use the guidance on pages 84–87 to help you plan your answer.

DO IT!

Make notes on different aspects of the relationship between Macbeth and Lady Macbeth. Look at how they communicate and try to influence each other. Complete the table for other parts of the play.

| Scene | Relationship between Macbeth and Lady Macbeth |
|---|---|
| Act 1, Scene 5 | Macbeth is reunited with his wife on returning home from war. She calls him 'great' perhaps to flatter him and make him easier to manipulate. He calls her 'dearest love' which probably expresses genuine love, making him more open to manipulation. |
| | |
| | |
| | |
| | |
| | |

# Character and theme essentials

## Macbeth

We learn a lot about Macbeth before we even meet him. In this way Shakespeare builds dramatic expectations in the audience. The Captain's battlefront report presents Macbeth as a hero who is savage and blood-thirsty in battle, showing no concern for his own safety, and Shakespeare does not signal that we should question this report. In fact, this heroic image of Macbeth is reinforced by Ross who attributes Scotland's victory to Macbeth.

## Lady Macbeth

Lady Macbeth is Macbeth's 'dearest partner of greatness' (Scene 5). She is determined to ensure Macbeth becomes king. She steels herself to help Macbeth murder Duncan, by calling on 'spirits' to replace her traditional female gentleness ('Unsex me here' – Scene 5) with 'direst cruelty' (Scene 5). She seems to actively seek evil. She is cunning enough to think up the perfect murder plan, and to gain Duncan's trust.

## Banquo

Banquo commanded the Scottish army with Macbeth. Duncan recognises that he has 'no less deserved' than Macbeth. He is loyal to Duncan and warns Macbeth against the evil influences of the witches.

## Duncan

Duncan is the King of Scotland. He rewards his thanes' loyalty and bravery with titles and with praise. However, he could be seen as over-trusting: he completely trusted Cawdor, and it might be that he is a poor judge of character, trusting too much to appearances.

## Evil and the supernatural

By opening the play with the witches, Shakespeare makes us fully aware of the evil forces that dominate the play's action. Shakespeare even has the witches celebrate evil and deception, 'Fair is foul, and foul is fair'. Their influence is implied in Macbeth's first words, that repeat the witches' words, 'So *foul and fair* a day I have not seen.' When Lady Macbeth also calls for obscurity – 'thick night' and 'the dunnest smoke of hell' (Scene 5) – perhaps Shakespeare is deliberately linking her to the witches.

## Ambition

Lady Macbeth worries that Macbeth does not have the 'illness' (wickedness and determination) to pursue their ambition to be 'great' (Scene 5) and powerful. Banquo and Macbeth react differently to the witches' predictions: Macbeth is immediately overwhelmed by the desire to become king.

## Trust and loyalty

Macbeth, Lady Macbeth and Banquo all treat Duncan to pledges of love and loyalty. We know that, in the case of the first two, these pledges are false.

## Appearance and reality

Duncan had 'an absolute trust' in the treacherous Cawdor (Scene 4) and concludes that you can't tell what someone is thinking by looking at their face. Yet both Duncan and Banquo seem to find in the 'face' of Macbeth's castle reassuring signs of trustworthiness (Scene 6). In contrast to Duncan, Lady Macbeth is sharply aware of the advantage of deception: 'Look like the 'innocent flower,/But be the serpent under it', she advises Macbeth (Scene 5).

**REVIEW IT!**

1 Your Shakespeare exam question is in Paper 1. Is it section A or section B?

2 How long should you spend on your Shakespeare question?

3 Where do the witches say they will meet Macbeth?

4 What is the name of the Scottish rebel who Macbeth kills in battle?

5 Why does Duncan call Macbeth 'valiant cousin! Worthy gentleman'?

6 When Ross describes Macbeth as 'lapp'd in proof', what does he mean?

7 Why is Duncan able to give Macbeth the title of Thane of Cawdor?

8 According to Banquo, how does Macbeth react to the witches' predictions for him?

9 What do the witches predict for Banquo?

10 Angus reports that the Thane of Cawdor lives 'under heavy judgement'. What does he mean by these words?

11 Macbeth thinks to himself, 'My thought, whose murder is yet fantastical...' What does he mean?

12 Why is Duncan amazed that Cawdor turned out to be a traitor?

13 When Macbeth is thinking about the title of Prince of Cumberland, what does he mean by his 'black and deep desires'?

14 When Lady Macbeth hears about the witches' 'promise', what does she fear about Macbeth?

15 What does Lady Macbeth mean when she asks spirits to 'unsex' her?

16 What important advice does Lady Macbeth give her husband in Scene 5?

17 Look at Duncan and Banquo's arrival at the Macbeths' castle. Write down four words and/or short **phrases** that show that the castle makes them feel safe and relaxed.

18 In his speech at the beginning of Scene 7, what reasons does Macbeth give for being reluctant to kill Duncan?

19 Lady Macbeth says that while her baby was smiling at her, she would 'Have pluck'd my nipple from his boneless gums/And dash'd the brains out...' Why does she say this, and what might be the effect of these words on an audience?

20 At the end of Scene 7, Macbeth decides to kill Duncan. What finally makes his mind up? ('I am settled')

# Act 2

## Act 2 Scene 1

### Summary: 'The heat-oppressed brain'

Banquo tells his son, Fleance, he is ready for bed except that he fears the 'cursed thoughts' of his dreams.

Macbeth arrives. Banquo tells Macbeth that the king was unusually happy before he went to bed. Banquo gives Macbeth a diamond for his wife. It is a present from the king. (Duncan calls Lady Macbeth 'most kind hostess' and has gone to bed 'in measureless content'.)

Macbeth says he hardly thinks about the witches' predictions but would welcome the chance to talk to Banquo about them. He promises that if he does become king, he will honour Banquo. Banquo and Fleance go. (Banquo warns Macbeth that he will only accept honours from King Macbeth if the crown has been won honourably. Does Banquo suspect Macbeth?)

Macbeth 'sees' a bloody dagger leading him towards Duncan. He realises he must get on with the murder before his intention cools.

## Act 2 Scene 2

### Summary: 'Macbeth shall sleep no more'

Lady Macbeth has drugged Duncan's guards. She hears Macbeth's voice and fears the guards have woken up. Macbeth enters. He has murdered Duncan. He says he could not say, 'Amen', when someone said, 'God bless us'. He fears he will never sleep again. (At this point in the play Lady Macbeth seems self-controlled. She has drunk enough to feel 'bold'. Macbeth seems stunned and horrified by what he has done.)

Lady Macbeth urges Macbeth to pull himself together and wash the blood from his hands. Then she realises he has brought the murder weapons with him. He refuses to return, so Lady Macbeth has to place the daggers next to the guards, whose faces she will smear with Duncan's blood. (Lady Macbeth planned the murder and she is just as clever about concealing the evidence.)

She returns with bloody hands, accuses Macbeth of cowardice and takes him away to wash their hands and go to bed. There is a constant knocking at the castle door.

### Mental torment

Macbeth and Lady Macbeth are being driven mad by the murder of Duncan. Just as Banquo is tormented by nightmares, so Macbeth is tormented by hallucinations, fears, guilt and – he predicts – lack of sleep.

Explore different images of mental torment as they are presented in Act 2 Scenes 1 and 2. Some images have been given to start you off. '…heat-oppressed brain' (Macbeth, Act 2 Scene 1), '…balm of hurt minds' (Macbeth, Act 2 Scene 2)

## Extract 1

Here Macbeth is hallucinating: he thinks he sees a dagger leading him to Duncan.

He does not know if he can trust his eyes. He even wonders if he has developed a sort of special 'supernatural sight' that involves visions.

> **MACBETH**
> Mine eyes are made the fools o' the other senses,
> Or else worth all the rest. I see thee still,
> And on thy blade and dudgeon gouts of blood,
> Which was not so before. There's no such thing:
> 5 It is the bloody business which informs
> Thus to mine eyes.

He knows that the pressure of being about to murder Duncan is playing tricks with his sight.

## DEFINE IT!

**balm** – something soothing; ointment

**but** – only

**dudgeon** – the hilt of a dagger (it protects the hand of the person holding the dagger)

**gout** – splash

**Neptune** – Roman god of the sea

## Extract 2

Thinking about the murder scene is bad enough, but seeing it makes it too real and horrifying for Macbeth. Eyes and what they see are closely linked to reality. Duncan's murdered body would be too *real* for Macbeth.

> **MACBETH**
> I am afraid to think what I have done;
> Look on't again I dare not.
>
> **LADY MACBETH**
> Infirm of purpose!
> Give me the daggers. The sleeping and the dead
> 5 Are but as pictures; 'tis the eye of childhood
> That fears a painted devil.

She scorns him for not looking calmly, and for imagining more than he sees. He sees evil but this evil is not real: it is only 'painted'.

Lady Macbeth says that death looks the same as sleep: they are the same 'picture'.

## Extract 3

> **MACBETH**
> What hands are here? Ha, they pluck out mine eyes!
> Will all great Neptune's ocean wash this blood
> Clean from my hand?

Macbeth's eyes seem to be sticking out in horror at the evidence of such a terrible crime. It also suggests again that light and sight are the enemies of evil, which relies on blindness and darkness.

 STRETCH IT!

How do visions and not being able to trust appearances become more significant later in the play?

## DO IT!

Explain the main differences between Macbeth's and Lady Macbeth's feelings about the scene of the murder.

How calm do you think Lady Macbeth is in this scene?

# Act 2 Scene 3

## Summary: 'Murder and treason!'

Grumbling and joking, the Porter finally opens the castle gate and admits Macduff and Lennox who have arrived to collect the king. (This is an unusual comic interlude in a very sinister, dramatic play. Think about what the play gains and/or loses by this episode with the Porter.)

While Macduff goes in to the king's chamber, Lennox tells Macbeth about the storm that raged through the night, and the supernatural noises they heard.

Macduff returns, horrified at Duncan's murder. He raises the alarm while Macbeth and Lennox go to see for themselves. Lady Macbeth expresses shock. (Notice how Lady Macbeth deflects any possible suspicion from herself.)

Macbeth and Lennox tell Donalbain and Malcolm of their father's murder, and Macbeth explains that he regrets not being able to resist killing the guards, who were clearly the killers. (Macbeth is clever: he has allowed the lords to see the 'evidence' of the guards' guilt, but then he has killed the only two witnesses.)

The lords agree to meet in the hall to discuss and investigate the murder. Donalbain and Malcolm agree that they, too, are at risk and decide to flee – Donalbain to Ireland, Malcolm to England. (Malcolm warns his brother that someone is showing fake outrage and 'unfelt sorrow', something that 'the false man does easy'. He clearly suspects that the real murderer is one of the lords.)

## Evil

Although the Porter is amusing, he does introduce himself as the gate-keeper of hell, which is actually Macbeth's castle. Lennox describes the evil, supernatural forces that raged while the murder was taking place, and his account is interrupted by Macduff's words, 'O horror, horror, horror!' The events of the play are full of classic ingredients of horror stories: witches, darkness, madness, evil.

## No going back

This scene is a crucial turning point in the development of the play's **plot**:

- the murder has been carried out and there is no going back

- Macbeth has changed from national hero to (secretly) treasonous murderer

- Macbeth and his wife have both acted to deflect suspicion from themselves

- Malcolm and Donalbain's escape allows them to prepare for revenge.

Choose another scene in the play that could be seen as a turning point where decisions or actions have a critical influence on the rest of the play's action.

Explain briefly why you consider that scene to be a turning point.

## Extract 1

In Act 1 Scene 7 Macbeth feared that murdering a gentle person like Duncan would be such a sin ('deep damnation') that the natural world would 'blow the horrid deed in every eye', giving away the murderer.

> **LENNOX**
> The night has been unruly. Where we lay,
> Our chimneys were blown down, and, as they say,
> Lamentings heard i'the air, strange screams of death,
> And prophesying with accents terrible
> 5 Of dire combustion and confused events
> New hatch'd to th'woeful time. The obscure bird
> Clamour'd the livelong night. Some say the earth
> Was feverous and did shake.
>
> **MACBETH**
> 'Twas a rough night.
>
> **LENNOX**
> 10 My young remembrance cannot parallel
> A fellow to it.
> *Re-enter MACDUFF*
>
> **MACDUFF**
> O horror, horror, horror! Tongue nor heart
> Cannot conceive nor name thee.

Lennox's description here might suggest that Macbeth's fearful prediction (above) has come true: Duncan's murder has triggered chaos, full of supernatural sounds and other terrifying phenomena.

Despite Macbeth's prediction apparently coming true, he seems to treat Lennox's report lightly. This might be because:

* he has toughened up
* he is trying to give an impression of calmness
* Lennox is well-known as boring or in the habit of exaggerating.

The repetition of this simple, powerful word conveys the genuineness of Macduff's feelings.

## DEFINE IT!

**clamour'd** – made a lot of noise

**combustion** – fire

**conceive** – imagine, understand

**feverous** – feverish, hot

**lamentings** – cries of grief

**obscure bird** – bird of the darkness: an owl

**prophesying** – making predictions for the future

**remembrance** – memory

## DO IT!

Make a short list of words and phrases that mean roughly the same as 'evil'. This list will help you when writing about this theme in the play. Here is one other word: 'sin'.

### AQA exam-style question

Starting with this extract, explore how Shakespeare presents a sense of horror in *Macbeth*.

Write about:

* how Shakespeare presents a sense of horror in this extract
* how Shakespeare presents a sense of horror in the play as a whole.

[30 marks]

Use the guidance on pages 84–87 to help you plan your answer.

## Act 2 Scene 4

### Summary: ''Tis unnatural'

'Somewhere in Scotland' Ross is talking to an Old Man about the strange and terrible things that have been happening to the natural world: the day is dark; the Old Man saw a falcon killed by an owl; Duncan's horses went wild, and attacked and 'eat [ate] each other'. (The natural order of things seems to have been upset by the murder of a king and a father – a doubly 'unnatural' act.)

Macduff arrives with the news that Duncan's sons appear to have paid the guards to kill their own father. Ross is shocked by this unnatural act. Macduff also reports that Macbeth has gone to Scone to be crowned king, and that Duncan has been buried with his predecessors.

Ross says he will go to the coronation, but Macduff says he is going home to Fife, suggesting he doesn't trust the official account of the murder. (Macduff sounds as though he doesn't trust Macbeth: he wants to keep his distance.)

The Old Man blesses them as they part. (Here is an example of the 'natural order' working properly: the Old Man is respected because of his age, and naturally expects to have his blessing welcomed by younger people.)

### A quiet moment in the play

The play is full of madness, chaos, plotting and violence. This scene is a rare quiet pause, coming straight after the dramatic, horrifying discovery of Duncan's murdered body. The Old Man and Ross are full of worry, but they consider the regicide and its aftermath calmly, thoughtfully. Perhaps this is another example of Shakespeare allowing his audience some 'breathing space' so as not to exhaust them with tension.

**DO IT!**

Many productions of *Macbeth* leave this short scene out.

EITHER Explain why you think this scene is important

OR Explain why you think this scene is unnecessary.

**STRETCH IT!**

Ross has not spoken since he met Macbeth and Banquo on the heath in Act 1 Scene 3. In some ways he is a mysterious **character**. Here are some interesting questions to consider:

- What did he think about Macbeth's reaction when he informed him that he was now Thane of Cawdor?

- What was Ross thinking when he arrived with Duncan at Macbeth's castle in Act 1 Scene 6?

- What is he thinking and feeling here in Act 2 Scene 4?

## Extract 1

'Father' was a term of respect for any respectable old man.

'Thou seest' is an old form of 'You see'.

> **ROSS**
> Ah, good father,
> Thou seest the heavens, as troubled with man's act,
> Threaten his bloody stage. By the clock 'tis day
> And yet dark night strangles the travelling lamp.
> 5 Is't night's predominance, or the day's shame,
> That darkness does the face of earth entomb,
> When living light should kiss it?

Ross fears that the sinful murder of a king (regicide) has angered God. The natural (and God-given) order has been challenged by humans.

The play's **imagery** is full of darkness and here – as elsewhere – darkness is linked to death, while light is linked to love and mercy.

**DO IT!**

Put Ross's words into your own words to make their meaning clear.

**DEFINE IT!**

**predominance** – greater strength

**ravin up** – devour, eat greedily

**thriftless** – wasteful

**travelling lamp** – the Sun (which appears to travel round the Earth)

## Extract 2

> **MACDUFF**
> Malcolm and Donalbain, the King's two sons,
> Are stol'n away and fled, which puts upon them
> Suspicion of the deed.
>
> **ROSS**
> 'Gainst nature still!
> 5 Thriftless ambition, that wilt ravin up
> Thine own life's means!…

Shakespeare often shortened -ed and -en word endings to 'n/'d, showing that the 'e' is not sounded. -ed was once sounded as a separate syllable. 'n indicates that the word is sounded as one syllable.

Ross is dismayed to think that the natural order has been so much offended: patricide is a deeply shocking crime. It is also wasteful because it involves destroying your own origin.

## Shakespeare's apostrophe

Shakespeare's **playscripts** often contain abbreviated words – words with a letter removed so as to take out one syllable. Here are some examples from the extracts above: ''tis' (it is); 'is't' (is it); 'stol'n' (stolen). Editors often assume that Shakespeare wanted to keep his lines of **verse** (poetry) to ten syllables; taking out a syllable was one way of making a line fit this pattern. Sometimes a ten-syllable line is split between two speeches or two speakers.

# Character and theme essentials

## Macbeth

Before, during and after Duncan's murder, Macbeth is in mental torment. His 'heat-oppressed brain' (Scene 2) makes him imagine a dagger leading him to Duncan's sleeping body. After the murder he is horrified by what he has done and fears he will 'sleep no more' (Scene 1). Despite his mental torment, he shows great self-control in front of Macduff and Lennox in order to divert suspicion away from himself and Lady Macbeth.

## Lady Macbeth

Lady Macbeth calls Macbeth 'Infirm of purpose!' (Scene 2). Ignoring doubts and hesitation is one of Lady Macbeth's key rules. She again shows herself to be a brilliant actor: she faints at the description of Duncan's murder scene. However, Shakespeare does **imply** Lady Macbeth struggles to suppress her underlying doubts and weaknesses: she can't murder Duncan herself because he 'resembled/My father as he slept' (Scene 2). This touching detail is another hint of Lady Macbeth's grief-stricken private life.

## Banquo

Again Banquo distances himself from any 'foul' means of making the witches' predictions come true: he tells Macbeth he won't do anything that will compromise his complete loyalty to Duncan.

## Macduff

Macduff is devastated by Duncan's murder, but he is also shocked by Macbeth's killing of the servants. There is a hint here that already he suspects Macbeth. His decision not to attend Macbeth's coronation but to return to his home hints more firmly at his suspicions.

## Evil and the supernatural

As Macbeth readies himself to murder Duncan, his language is full of references to witchcraft and darkness. He welcomes a sense of 'present horror' (Scene 1) because it suits what he is about to do. An atmosphere of the supernatural runs throughout the murder scene, enhanced by Lady Macbeth being startled by the sound of an owl shrieking – a traditional accompaniment for scenes of horror.

## Sin

Macduff calls Duncan's murder, 'sacrilegious' – an offence against God that has involved breaking into 'The Lord's anointed temple'. This extended holy **metaphor** emphasises the sinfulness of the murder, not just its illegality. The Porter – although comic – is presented as the gate-keeper of hell, which here is Macbeth's castle.

## Men and women

Again, Lady Macbeth outdoes Macbeth in some 'manly' characteristics: notably in her ability to suppress any sense of guilt. On the other hand, other characters' traditional assumptions about women's 'gentleness' leave her free from suspicion.

## Appearance and reality

The hiding and falsifying of evidence is the Macbeths' way of ensuring that other characters accept appearance as reality. The simplicity of Lady Macbeth's tactics is impressive: 'A little water clears us of this deed', she explains to Macbeth. She means that if they wash the blood from their hands they will appear to be innocent.

## Chaos and nature

'Nature seems dead' Macbeth remarks as he prepares to murder Duncan (Scene 1). Ross calls the murder ''Gainst Nature' – especially if it was committed by Duncan's own sons. This attack on nature causes chaos: horses eating each other, and so on. Perhaps Shakespeare is reflecting the country's anxiety over disorder threatened by alarming events such as the gunpowder plot.

**REVIEW IT!**

1 What does Banquo give Macbeth from Duncan?
2 What vision does Macbeth have after Banquo leaves?
3 Where does the vision seem to be leading Macbeth?
4 What reason does Lady Macbeth give for not killing Duncan herself?
5 What unsettled Macbeth when he had killed Duncan?
6 What does Lady Macbeth mean by 'brain-sickly' thinking?
7 What does Lady Macbeth mean when she says, 'A little water clears us of this deed'?
8 What place does the Porter imagine himself to be gate-keeping?
9 Why does Macduff call at Macbeth's castle so early?
10 How does Macduff connect Duncan's murder to sin, not just a crime?
11 Why is Macduff reluctant to tell Lady Macbeth what has happened?
12 What is Macbeth's excuse for having killed Duncan's guards?
13 Why do Duncan's sons decide to run away?
14 Ross tells the Old Man, 'Thou seest the heavens, as troubled with man's act'. State three ways that heaven has shown itself to be 'troubled' by Duncan's murder.
15 Why do you think Macduff decides not to attend Macbeth's coronation?
16 In Scene 1, what does Macbeth mean by 'Words to the heat of deeds too cold breath gives'?
17 In what ways is Lady Macbeth more self-controlled than her husband after the murder of Duncan?
18 How well does Macbeth divert suspicion from himself when Duncan's murder is discovered?
19 What do you make of Ross from what he says in Scene 4?
20 If someone had never before seen or read *Macbeth,* what might they expect to happen after the end of Act 2? Would they expect the Macbeths to get away with their crime? Give reasons for your thoughts.

# Act 3

## Act 3 Scene 1

### Summary: 'Our fears in Banquo stick deep'

Banquo suspects that Macbeth 'play'dst most foully' to become king, but he hopes that the witches' predictions for him will also come true. (Banquo and Macbeth are close friends. Why do you think Banquo suspects Macbeth?)

Macbeth insists that Banquo returns from his afternoon ride in time for the evening's 'supper'. Left alone, Macbeth expresses his fear of Banquo's bravery, wisdom and – by implication – his suspicion. He burns with resentment that it is Banquo's children who will follow him as kings, leaving Macbeth with a 'fruitless crown'. (Macbeth can't bear the idea that Banquo's children will gain from Macbeth's murder of Duncan, an act that 'filed my mind'. This graphic metaphor highlights the agony Macbeth has inflicted on himself by murdering Duncan.')

Macbeth has a private meeting with two men he spoke with the previous day. He persuades them to murder Banquo and his son, Fleance, by reminding them that Banquo is their enemy who has oppressed and impoverished them. He suggests that if they are real men – and not just men in name – they will kill their oppressor and earn Macbeth's love. (Note how crafty and manipulative Macbeth is in his persuasion.)

Macbeth explains that although Banquo is his enemy too, he cannot afford to be linked to Banquo's murder. The two men agree to murder Banquo after Macbeth promises to tell them where 'to plant' themselves so as to carry out the operation successfully.

### Shakespeare the playwright

Shakespeare is often thought of as a poet and a philosopher whose ideas are 'deep'. However, Shakespeare was first of all a **playwright** whose scripts had to help actors to engage an audience. The opening of this scene shows an expert **dramatist** at work. Look at how he has Macbeth end his conversation with Banquo three times, only to throw in an innocent-sounding question to Banquo as though as an after-thought. This technique leaves the audience to develop a growing awareness of Macbeth's real intentions: he is seeking the information he needs to plan Banquo's murder. Of course, the actor can also deliver these questions in a way that worries and even intimidates Banquo. Shakespeare has designed this scene with great subtlety.

### STRETCH IT!

Re-read Macbeth's conversation with the murderers. Explain how Macbeth uses insinuation to persuade them.

32

## Extract 1

The murderers are ordinary people whose hardships are immediate and basic – poverty, hunger, lack of freedom. The hard alliteration of the 'b' sound directly conveys the physical reality of their hardship.

> **SECOND MURDERER**
> I am one, my liege,
> Whom the vile blows and buffets of the world
> Have so incensed that I am reckless what
> I do to spite the world.
>
> **FIRST MURDERER**
> 5 And I another
> So weary with disasters, tugg'd with fortune,
> That I would set my life on any chance,
> To mend it or be rid on't.

The first murderer's reply is compressed to again emphasise how immediate and inescapable their misfortune is. (He says little more than 'me too'.) His words' blunt **monosyllables** further emphasise the absolute barrenness of their lives: there is nothing to be poetic about.

## Extract 2

The simple, direct way the murderers speak again emphasises that they have no doubts about carrying out Macbeth's plan.

> **MURDERERS**
> We are resolved, my lord.
>
> **MACBETH**
> I'll call upon you straight. Abide within.
>
> *Exeunt* MURDERERS
> It is concluded: Banquo, thy soul's flight,
> 5 If it find heaven, must find it out tonight.

Macbeth's reply is equally direct and businesslike.

Macbeth's decisiveness is confirmed in the neatness of these two lines. Shakespeare often used rhyming couplets to signal to the audience an important moment, or a section or scene.

**DO IT!**
Write three more lines about one example of Shakespeare's use of language in this scene.

Here a student is writing about how Macbeth persuades the murderers. Look closely at how this student examines the effect of Shakespeare's choice of language.

The student defines the style used.

The student identifies the reason for Shakespeare's choice of style.

The murderer says, 'I am reckless what I do...' This direct and colloquial language implies how desperate the man is. It is not elaborate or poetic, and that is fitting because his own life is not elaborate or poetic, but a harsh, physical struggle to survive.

**DEFINE IT!**

buffets – blows, shakes

exeunt - a stage direction telling all the characters to leave the stage

fruitless – barren, sterile, not having children

liege – Lord

resolv'd – your mind is made up

## Act 3 Scene 2

### Summary: 'Full of scorpions is my mind, dear wife!'

Lady Macbeth tells Macbeth there is no point in brooding on his own about what they have done. 'What's done is done', she tells him. Macbeth longs for safety, especially from Duncan's sons. (What Lady Macbeth does not know is that Macbeth has been arranging the murder of Banquo and Fleance on his own.)

Lady Macbeth tells her husband to be 'bright and jovial' and he asks her to treat Banquo with great respect at the evening's feast. Macbeth longs to be able to stop hiding his real feelings. (At this point Macbeth already knows that Banquo will be dead before the evening, so why does he ask his wife to pay Banquo respect at the feast?)

Again Lady Macbeth urges him to stop worrying, but he now expresses a new worry – that Banquo and his son are alive. She soothes him by pointing out that they won't live forever. Macbeth tells her he has planned 'A deed of dreadful note', but he refuses to give her any more detail. ('What's to be done?' Lady Macbeth asks Macbeth in surprise. Although Macbeth treated his wife as a close partner at every step of the murder of Duncan, he doesn't even consult her about his plans for Banquo.)

He says that their evil act has brought them problems that can only be solved by more evil.

### Night and day

Night and day and light and dark feature as dramatic contrasts throughout the play. In this scene, night is evil's natural habitat and night is even **personified** by Macbeth as a cruel killer whose 'bloody and invisible hand' will slaughter Banquo and Fleance. To link night closely to fear, Shakespeare threads Macbeth's speech with a series of images of death and the occult including 'black Hecate's summons', 'night's yawning peal' and 'night's black agents'. For Macbeth, night's great advantage is that it conceals, making attack easier and detection harder. By contrast, day is personified as being 'pitiful' with its 'tender eye'.

Find another part of the play where night or darkness is described.

Explain how night (or darkness) is presented in that scene. What does it symbolise?

You could make your own choice, or you could write about this section:

Act 2 Scene 3: Lennox's speech that begins, 'The night has been unruly…'

## Extract 1

Lady Macbeth handles Macbeth in various ways. Here she soothes and reassures him.

> Here Macbeth is deceiving Lady Macbeth: he is implying that Banquo will be alive to attend the feast.

> Macbeth points out the need to disguise their real thoughts and plans. This constant pretence is an unfortunate burden.
> A 'vizard' is the mask of a battle helmet. This metaphor implies that their 'false faces' not only disguise their feelings, but *protect* them too, thus conveying Macbeth's sense of *vulnerability*.

> **LADY MACBETH**
> Come on,
> Gentle my lord, sleek o'er your rugged looks;
> Be bright and jovial among your guests tonight.
>
> **MACBETH**
> So shall I, love, and so, I pray, be you.
> 5 Let your remembrance apply to Banquo;
> Present him eminence, both with eye and tongue:
> Unsafe the while, that we
> Must lave our honours in these flattering streams
> And make our faces vizards to our hearts,
> 10 Disguising what they are.
>
> **LADY MACBETH**
> You must leave this.
>
> **MACBETH**
> O, full of scorpions is my mind, dear wife!
> Thou know'st that Banquo and his Fleance lives.
>
> **LADY MACBETH**
> But in them nature's copy's not eterne.

> 'Sleek' is an **adjective**, but here Shakespeare uses it as a verb – a good example of one aspect of his creative approach to language: he invents new words or uses words in new ways. 'Sleek' and 'rugged' are opposites.

> This startling metaphor powerfully expresses Macbeth's mental torment and emphasises the contrast between his real thoughts and feelings, and the impression he gives to others.

### DO IT!

Explain how deception is presented in the following quotation from Act 2 Scene 2:

Find and note down at least two more brief quotations in which deception is presented.

> I'll gild the faces of the grooms withal,
> For it must seem their guilt.

## AQA exam-style question

Starting with this conversation, explore how Shakespeare presents concealment and deception in *Macbeth.*

Write about:

- how Shakespeare presents concealment and deception in this conversation

- how far Shakespeare presents concealment and deception in the play as a whole.

[30 marks]

Use the guidance on pages 84–87 to help you plan your answer.

### DEFINE IT!

**eterne** – eternal, going on forever

**Hecate** – the goddess of witchcraft

**jovial** – cheerful

**lave** – wash, clean

**occult** – the supernatural (usually evil)

**peal** – the sound made by a church bell

**vizard** – mask

## Act 3 Scene 3

### Summary: 'Who did bid thee join with us?'

To their surprise the two Murderers are joined by a third man who says Macbeth has sent him. (The Third Murderer is an intriguing mystery that is never explained.)

They ambush and murder Banquo but his son, Fleance, escapes.

### The Third Murderer

Who is the Third Murderer? He says he has been sent by Macbeth. Has Macbeth sent him to ensure the Murderers do their job? If so, who would Macbeth trust with this task? Is he lying when he says Macbeth sent him? If so, how did he know about the murder plot? Did he overhear Macbeth's meeting with the Murderers? In which case why hasn't he given Macbeth away? What do you think?

## Act 3 Scene 4

### Summary: 'Never shake thy gory locks at me!'

As Macbeth is welcoming the lords to his feast, the First Murderer tells him they failed to kill Fleance. Macbeth is dismayed but dismisses the Murderer, telling him they will meet the next day. (Many productions of the play suggest that Macbeth has the Murderers murdered.)

Macbeth is about to sit down when he sees Banquo's ghost in his place. No one else can see the ghost. Lady Macbeth excuses Macbeth's crazed reaction as a fit that has suffered from youth. She reassures him that his imagination is playing tricks on him, but he continues to rave. (Lady Macbeth tries to control Macbeth by shaming him for being unmanly: his fears are as unreal as 'a woman's story at a winter's fire.' She accuses him of being 'unmann'd in folly.')

He has just controlled himself and confirmed Lady Macbeth's explanation of his 'strange infirmity' when he sees the ghost again. Lady Macbeth tells everyone to leave immediately because Macbeth 'grows worse and worse'.

Macbeth tells Lady Macbeth of his fear that his secrets are being exposed. He says he will spy on Macduff and consult the witches, so that he can 'know...the worst'. (Although Macbeth is losing control of himself, he is still plotting and planning coldly.) Lady Macbeth tells him he just needs sleep. (Macbeth cannot sleep because by murdering Duncan, he 'murder'd sleep'.)

## Extract 1

Here Macbeth is speaking to Banquo's ghost.

Compare this with Macbeth's earlier protest to his wife: 'I dare do all that may become a man;/Who dares do more is none.' (Act 1 Scene 7) Being a man includes being brave and even blood-thirsty, but that is not enough.

A ghost

**MACBETH**
What man dare, I dare.
Approach thou like the rugged Russian bear,
The arm'd rhinoceros, or the Hyrcan tiger;
Take any shape but that, and my firm nerves
5 Shall never tremble. Or be alive again,
And dare me to the desert with thy sword;
If trembling I inhabit then, protest me
The baby of a girl. Hence, horrible shadow!
Unreal mockery, hence!

10 *Exit* GHOST

Why, so, being gone,
I am a man again.

It is manly to fight real, physical creatures or forces that are too strong to defeat, but being terrified of the supernatural is acceptable even for a man.

He would fight Banquo if he were alive.

What does Macbeth mean by this? Does he mean that once the challenge of a ghost has gone, he can 'be' a man again? He can be seen as the brave warrior that everyone thinks he is.

A doll. This image suggests cowardice would make Macbeth 'worse' than a girl: he would be under the control of a girl.

## Context

How a modern audience reacts is a valid aspect of **context**. Shakespeare seems very deliberately to sow the text with references to manliness and womanliness and how Lady Macbeth often seems to exhibit manly strengths more than Macbeth does. Yet how Shakespeare might have expected his own audiences to react to this issue is unclear. Certainly most modern audiences will respond from a point of view that values equality between the sexes, a perspective that would be unfamiliar to Shakespeare's audiences.

**DEFINEIT!**

hence – from here

**Hyrcan tiger** – Hyrcania was in what is now Iran; Hyrcanian tigers were thought to be especially fierce

**NAILIT!**

In your AQA exam, it is OK to explore your personal response, but do explain your views with reference to details in the text.

To show that you are exploring *possible* interpretations, use tentative words such as 'perhaps', 'this could/might', 'suggest/imply'.

**DOIT!**

Is Macbeth unmanly?

Does it matter how manly he is?

In what ways is Lady Macbeth more 'manly' than Macbeth?

## Act 3 Scene 5

### Summary: 'How now, Hecate?'

The powerful witch, Hecate, tells off the three witches for helping a man - Macbeth – who does not deserve it, and for not involving her. She tells them that she will be taking charge from this point. It is unlikely that Shakespeare wrote this short scene. It was probably inserted at a later date by another playwright.

## Act 3 Scene 6

### Summary: 'Our suffering country'

Lennox is talking to another Lord, reviewing recent events and observing how conveniently things have turned out for Macbeth. He seems to imply that he does not trust the official account of Duncan's murder. He asks the Lord if he knows where Macduff has gone. (Lennox is very careful in his speech. He is probably being sarcastic about Macbeth's explanations, but perhaps he is genuinely unsure what to think. Some productions suggest that Lennox is trying to win the Lord's trust in order to get important information from him.)

The Lord reports that Macduff has gone to seek military help in England where Duncan's son, Malcolm, has been welcomed. The Lord hopes that an army will invade Scotland and restore freedom to the Scottish people. (The Lord is clear in his view that, with Macbeth as king, they are living under a tyranny and they 'pine for' liberation.)

The Lord reports that Macbeth has requested Macduff to return, but Macduff has refused. Lennox hopes that an English army will bring 'a swift blessing' to their 'suffering country'.

### Structure

Both these scenes give information about events that we have not seen. The short Hecate scene tells us how the supernatural world views Macbeth. The tone and style of this scene seems trivial, jarring with the rest of the play. That alone suggests the scene is not an original part of the play, but added later.

The Lennox and the Lord scene is more useful. It tells us that:

- Macbeth's account of the death of Duncan does not convince everyone
- Scotland has fallen into chaos and misery under Macbeth's rule
- Macbeth cannot count on the automatic loyalty of his lords any more than Duncan could.

### Kingship

Macbeth's tyranny is contrasted with the good kingship of 'the most pious Edward', the English king.

Find at least one other part of the play which summarises or comments on events.

What do we learn from that part of the play?

## Extract 1

Lennox is guarded: he suggests that his doubts are only the Lord's 'interpretation'. His next word, 'only', signals to the Lord that he is not committed to what he might be implying.

This is another example of Lennox's method of not **explicitly** committing to what he is implying: it is only an accusation *if it pleases* the hearer – if they **interpret** it that way.

> **LENNOX**
> My former speeches have but hit your thoughts,
> Which can interpret further; only I say things have
> been strangely borne. The gracious Duncan
> Was pitied of Macbeth; marry, he was dead.
> 5 And the right valiant Banquo walk'd too late,
> Whom, you may say, if't please you, Fleance kill'd,
> For Fleance fled. Men must not walk too late.
> Who cannot want the thought, how monstrous
> It was for Malcolm and for Donalbain
> 10 To kill their gracious father? Damned fact!
> How it did grieve Macbeth! Did he not straight,
> In pious rage, the two delinquents tear
> That were the slaves of drink and thralls of sleep?
> Was not that nobly done? Ay, and wisely too.

Throughout the speech Lennox implies disbelief in Macbeth's explanations, but then follows each detail with an unlikely reason for believing it.

The overall effect is that Lennox sounds sarcastic without directly accusing Macbeth.

## DEFINE IT!

**delinquent** – someone who breaks the law

**kingship** – ruling as a king

**pious** – religious; devoted to god

**thralls** – slaves

**tyranny** – a government that rules through force and fear, tolerating no opposition

**valiant** – brave

### AQA exam-style question

Starting with this speech, explore how Shakespeare presents one or more of the minor lords as commentators on the action.

Choose from Lennox, Ross, Angus or the unnamed 'Lord' in this scene.

Write about:

- how Shakespeare presents Lennox as commentator in this speech
- how Shakespeare presents minor lords as commentators in the play as a whole.

[30 marks]

Use the guidance on pages 84–87 to help you plan your answer.

## STRETCH IT!

To gain the highest marks in your answer in your AQA exam you need to develop a 'conceptual response' to the question. That means starting with a clear and thoughtful point of view. Here is an example:

Lennox could just be a convenient device Shakespeare uses to summarise important off-stage action, but it is fascinating how often his news is likely to unsettle the hearer - especially Macbeth. Could Shakespeare be using him as a sort of agent provocateur? Perhaps Lennox doesn't just report events but craftily implies a comment on those events. Could an actor present him in that way?

## NAILIT!

In your AQA exam, it is important not to treat characters as though they are real people. They have been deliberately created and shaped by the writer. How a reader reacts to the character is an important part of how the writer *presents* them.

# Character and theme essentials

## Macbeth

Macbeth is being driven mad by lack of sleep, guilt, the terror of being found out, and – of course - by horrific hallucinations. He is becoming increasingly erratic and crazed as he coldly plots to assassinate his rivals. He is now proceeding without consulting his wife.

## Lady Macbeth

Lady Macbeth is starting to feel abandoned and isolated, and is beginning to wish she was dead, instead of suffering their 'doubtful joy' (Scene 2). Her determination to survive is shown in the way she manages Macbeth and his outbursts.

## Banquo

Banquo suspects that Macbeth has 'play'dst most foully' to become king. In the story Shakespeare used as his source for *Macbeth*, Banquo helps Macbeth to kill Duncan. The play was first performed in front of King James 1 who was a descendant of Banquo, so probably Shakespeare decided to make his Banquo a 'goodie' so as not to offend the king.

## Lennox

Lennox is mysterious. He hopes that Scotland can quickly be freed from Macbeth's 'accursed hand'. However, a recent major production of the play suggested Lennox is an agent of Macbeth, tempting the Lord to reveal information about Macduff. In that production Lennox murders the Lord at the end of the act. Other productions have had Lennox fill the role of the Third Murderer.

## Evil and the supernatural

Macbeth's language at the end of Scene 2 is full of occult imagery, as though Macbeth is working up an evil spell. In addition, his long speeches are spell-binding, hypnotic. For example:

> Light thickens, and the crow
> Makes wing to the rooky wood;
> Good things of day begin to droop and drowse,
> Whiles night's black agents to their preys do rouse.

The listener is spellbound by:

- the hushed, but insistent movement of these words

- the string of unsettling and original images ('Light thickens', 'rooky wood')

- the alliteration of '**dr**oop and **dr**owse'

- the rhyming couplet ('drowse'/'rouse').

## Kingship

In Shakespeare's time, no monarch was entirely safe: their power was often challenged by other powerful people in the country and abroad. In return for their support, the king was expected to defend his people and rule in their interests. Clearly Macbeth breaks this traditional 'contract' with his people.

## Men and women

Again in this act, men are controlled by being accused of unmanliness. Lady Macbeth uses this tactic to get Macbeth to pull himself together at the feast. Macbeth uses it to shame two desperate men to kill Banquo for him.

1  What does Banquo plan to do until Macbeth's feast?

2  What does Macbeth say he will do until the feast?

3  What two strengths does Macbeth fear in Banquo?

4  How does Macbeth try to shame the Murderers?

5  What reason does Macbeth give for not killing Banquo himself?

6  When Macbeth arrives to speak to Lady Macbeth, what advice does she give him?

7  What does Macbeth tell Lady Macbeth to 'be innocent of'?

8  What do the Murderers suspect to be Macbeth's reason for sending a Third Murderer to kill Banquo?

9  What reason does Macbeth give to his guests for not sitting down at the start of the feast?

10  How does Macbeth comfort himself over Fleance's escape from the Murderers?

11  What does Macbeth mean when he says that Banquo's absence he would 'rather challenge for unkindness/Than pity for mischance!'?

12  What is Lady Macbeth's explanation for Macbeth's behaviour after he has seen Banquo's ghost?

13  How does Lady Macbeth try to shame Macbeth into controlling himself?

14  What does Macbeth find astonishing about his wife's calm reactions?

15  When their guests have left, what cure does Lady Macbeth suggest for Macbeth's madness?

16  Scene 6: List at least two brief quotations from Lennox's first speech that could be read as sarcasm.

17  Scene 1: What does Banquo think about Macbeth, and how do we know?

18  Scene 2: Macbeth explains his worry to Lady Macbeth in his words, 'We have scotch'd the snake, not kill'd it.' What does he mean by this metaphor?

19  At the end of Scene 5, Macbeth tells Lady Macbeth:

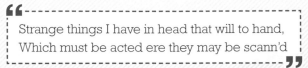

> Strange things I have in head that will to hand,
> Which must be acted ere they may be scann'd

What is the significance of these words?

20  At the end of Act 3, Lennox describes Scotland as a 'suffering country/Under a hand accursed!' What evidence is there in Act 3 to support Lennox's description of Scotland?

# Act 4

## Act 4 Scene 1

### Summary: 'Macbeth! Macbeth! Macbeth! Beware Macduff'

Waiting for Macbeth's visit, the witches mix up a potion in their cauldron. The witches call up ghosts to tell Macbeth that he should 'beware Macduff', but that he can never be beaten by any man 'of woman born' and even then not until Birnam Wood moves to Dunsinane Hill. Macbeth is relieved by this, but decides to kill Macduff to make sure he is no threat. (Note that Macduff's threat and Macbeth's suspicions of him strengthen throughout the play. By this point Shakespeare has made the audience expect a final 'showdown' between the two men.)

When Macbeth asks if Banquo's sons will be kings, the witches show him visions of eight kings and Banquo's ghost 'points at them for his'. The last king holds a glass reflecting 'many more' Banquo descendants into the future, some carrying symbols of dual kingship (presumably Scotland *and* England). (King James 1 was king of Scotland during the time Shakespeare was writing; he was also a descendant of Banquo. Presumably, Shakespeare was flattering him with this suggestion that his kingship was rightful, inevitable and safe.)

The witches vanish and Lennox arrives with the news that Macduff has 'fled to England'. Macbeth vows in the future to carry out his thoughts without delay. He decides to have Macduff's family slaughtered immediately. (Macbeth keeps warning himself to act quickly and decisively. As early as Act 2 Scene 1 he realised that 'Words to the heat of deeds too cold breath gives.')

## Macbeth

Macbeth knows he has reached the point where there is no turning back. In this scene he is determined to hear the worst so that he can take the right steps to strengthen his position. As his wife advised him earlier, 'Things without all remedy/Should be without regard' (Act 3 Scene 2). In other words, there is no point in wishing that he did something different in the past. They did what they did. He accepts this point when he realises that 'Things bad begun make strong themselves by ill.' (Act 3 Scene 2) Once you have gone down the path of evil you have to continue.

1 Make a list of the ways in which Macbeth shows his determination and courage in this scene. Consider:
   • how he speaks to the witches
   • how he seeks information even when he fears it
   • the bravado in the way he responds to what he learns.

2 Think about how *you* would think and feel if you were in Macbeth's position.

## Extract 1

Macbeth rejects the witches' warning.

**MACBETH**

That will never be.
Who can impress the forest, bid the tree
Unfix his earth-bound root? Sweet bodements, good!
Rebellion's head, rise never till the Wood
5 Of Birnam rise, and our high-placed Macbeth
Shall live the lease of nature, pay his breath
To time and mortal custom. Yet my heart
Throbs to know one thing: tell me, if your art
Can tell so much, shall Banquo's issue ever
10 Reign in this kingdom?

**ALL THE WITCHES**

Seek to know no more.

**MACBETH**

I will be satisfied. Deny me this,
And an eternal curse fall on you. Let me know.

The lines in this speech are in **iambic pentameter**. The tidy rhythm of these lines gives Macbeth's words confidence and decisiveness. This effect is strengthened by the rhyming couplets. However, **enjambement** softens this decisive tone by preventing most of the rhymes from being stressed.

The short sentences and imperative verbs again emphasise Macbeth's determination.

## DEFINE IT!

**bodements** – omens, predictions

**impress** – force

**issue** – children

**lease of nature** – a normal lifespan

# Iambic pentameter

Iambs give a line a dee-*dum*, dee-*dum* regular rhythm. However, if all lines were spoken with an inflexible 'dee-dum' rhythm then their subtlety and meaning would become lost, and the effect would be very tiresome for the audience. Actors must decide which syllables should be stressed for meaning. (See also page 82.)

## NAIL IT!

In your AQA exam, it is better to think of iambic pentameter as the underlying form of Shakespeare's poetry, rather than being a strict rule.

## STRETCH IT!

Find a place where the playscript switches from **prose** to verse (or the other way round). Read aloud the lines either side of the switch. Ask yourself these questions:

- Why do you think Shakespeare switched between forms here (see page 82)?

- How does the tone of the scene change after the switch?

You could choose Act 3 Scene 4 from Macbeth, 'Ourself will mingle…', down to Macbeth, 'The table round.'.

## AQA exam-style question

Starting with this speech, explore how Shakespeare presents Macbeth as a brave man in *Macbeth*.

Write about:

- how Shakespeare presents Macbeth in this extract

- how Shakespeare presents Macbeth as a brave man in the play as a whole.

[30 marks]

Use the guidance on pages 84–87 to help you plan your answer.

# Act 4 Scene 2

## Summary: 'He has kill'd me, Mother'

Ross visits his cousin, Lady Macduff. He tries to defend Macduff's decision to leave his family unprotected. Lady Macduff accuses Macduff of fear, and lack of wisdom and love. Ross explains that Macduff is wise enough to know 'The fits o' the season' – Macduff understands the dangerous state of Scotland at this time. (Lady Macduff does not meekly accept that her husband must be doing the right thing: she condemns him. Although her part in the play is very small, Lady Macduff comes across as a strong woman.)

When Ross leaves, Lady Macduff tells her son his father is dead and a traitor. Her son scorns both claims. (Lady Macduff is amused by her son's logic, and her response shows her love for him: 'Poor prattler, how thou talk'st!' By creating a mood of affection here, Shakespeare makes the boy's murder even more shocking and brutal.)

A messenger arrives to warn Lady Macduff that 'danger does approach'. As he leaves, unknown men arrive and kill Lady Macduff's son. The men chase Lady Macduff as she shouts 'murder!' (We don't know who the messenger is: Shakespeare teases us with this mystery.)

**STRETCH**IT!

What might be gained or lost by leaving this scene out?

## Writing about the effect of structure

Below is part of a student's writing about the **structure** of this scene and how it fits into the play.

The student is trying to:

- write in a critical style appropriate to analysing the effect of this scene on the audience

- use evidence properly and usefully.

> At the end of the scene before, Macbeth says he has at last learned that the very firstlings of his heart must be the firstlings of his hand, so Shakespeare proves this by making the next scene the murder - Macbeth doing what he said he'd do straight away.

- How well has the student done the two things they set out to do?
- What could they have done to improve their writing?

For further guidance, refer to the mark scheme improvement descriptors on page 86.

## Doing without the scene

Some productions of *Macbeth* leave out this scene, believing that it is not essential: we already know that Macduff has fled to England and in the next scene Ross spares no details of the murder: 'your wife and babes/Savagely slaughter'd,' he tells Macduff. Some even say that the play is better without this scene.

## Extract 1

Lady Macduff accuses her husband of cowardice: to 'fly' means to run away, and she uses the word 'babes' instead of 'children' to stress how defenceless they are.

> **LADY MACDUFF**
> Wisdom? To leave his wife, to leave his babes,
> His mansion, and his titles, in a place
> From whence himself does fly? He loves us not;

Lady Macduff's independence is confirmed in her rhetorical language here. She begins her central accusation in very short questions (the first just one word) and then goes on to convey her firmness and her scorn for Ross's explanation.

The whole rhetorical question gathers momentum until it stops abruptly. The following phrase comprises monosyllables to punch out the conclusion.

The main accusation repeats the construction, 'to leave his', as though she is making a convincing speech.

## Extract 2

Ross feels restricted in what he dares say. Presumably he knows there is no house where Macbeth does not 'keep a servant feed' – bribed to be a spy (Act 3 Scene 4).

> **ROSS**
> I dare not speak much further;
> But cruel are the times when we are traitors
> And do not know ourselves; when we hold rumour
> From what we fear, yet know not what we fear,
> 5 But float upon a wild and violent sea
> Each way and move.

From this we learn that Scotland is in the grip of fear and rumour, and people are forced through fear of Macbeth to act against their own beliefs.

In this metaphor, 'float' suggests that Ross – and other Scots – have no control. The 'wild and violent sea' could be Macbeth's behaviour, and his method of rule over the country.

## DO IT!

Read Ross's words in extract 2 and the notes alongside. Write a paragraph in answer to these two questions:

1 To what are Ross and other Scots 'traitors'?

2 What point is Ross trying to make to Lady Macduff in this speech?

## DEFINE IT!

**prattler** – someone who chatters without much purpose

**traitor** – someone who goes against his country, friends or principles

**whence** – where

## Act 4 Scene 3

### Summary: 'Your wife and babes savagely slaughter'd'

Macduff is talking to Malcolm in the English court. Macduff is asking Malcolm to return with him to Scotland at the head of an army. Macduff despairs when Malcolm refuses, saying that he does not entirely trust Macduff. He then tells Macduff that as a king he – Malcolm – would be even more evil than Macbeth, who would look 'pure as snow' by comparison. He says he is full of lust and greed and has none of the 'graces' that a king should have. (Malcolm pretends that he will use the absolute power of the throne for his own ends.)

Macduff is outraged, calling Malcolm's description of himself a blasphemy against his own saintly parents. Now Malcolm reveals that he was pretending, his purpose being to test whether Macduff could be trusted. He tells Macduff that a 10,000-strong army commanded by English Earl Old Siward is ready to invade Scotland. (Malcolm calls Macduff's passionate reaction to his self-condemnation proof of his 'integrity' (honesty).)

Malcolm tells Macduff that the English king, Edward, seems to have the ability to heal people who are suffering from the evil (scrofula).

Ross arrives and reports that Scotland is now like a grave. Then he tells Macduff of the murder of his wife, children and servants. Macduff is shocked but Malcolm tells him the only cure for his grief is revenge. Macduff vows to kill Macbeth. (Malcolm tells Macduff to take the news of his family's murder 'like a man'.)

### Dramatic structure

Productions sometimes leave out this scene up to Ross's arrival. Some directors consider it too slow and wordy just when the play should be building to a climax. However, in the first half of this scene we learn about an important effect of Macbeth's rule: no one can afford to trust anyone else without testing them out. As well as murdering sleep (see Act 2 Scene 2), Macbeth has also 'murdered' trust.

### Kingship

We also learn more about what was expected of a 'good' king: 'justice, verity, temperance, stableness, bounty, perseverance, mercy, lowliness, devotion, patience, courage, fortitude'. In addition, both Malcolm's murdered father, Duncan, and the English king, Edward the Confessor, are praised as godly men. Was Shakespeare presenting his own king, James I, with reminders about what was expected of him? Or perhaps Shakespeare wanted to flatter James by implying that James already had all these virtues.

## Extract 1

Malcolm orders Macduff to take ('dispute') his tragic news 'like a man'. He does not suggest Macduff should suppress his feelings (he has already warned against that): he means Macduff should not let those feelings overwhelm him.

Macduff's words and reactions show that expressing emotions is part of being a man.

**MALCOLM**
Dispute it like a man.

**MACDUFF**
I shall do so,
But I must also feel it as a man.
I cannot but remember such things were
5 That were most precious to me. Did heaven look on,
And would not take their part? Sinful Macduff,
They were all struck for thee! Naught that I am,
Not for their own demerits, but for mine,
Fell slaughter on their souls. Heaven rest them now!

**MALCOLM**
10 Be this the whetstone of your sword. Let grief
Convert to anger, blunt not the heart, enrage it.

Macduff believes heaven has punished him for the sin of leaving his family unprotected.

Malcolm speaks in a series of commands, fronted with imperative verbs. This conveys his kingly authority. His authority is strengthened by the proverb-like quality of his words, making them sound like ancient wisdoms. 'Whetstone' here is a metaphor for the grief (and anger) that will 'sharpen' Macduff's sword by inspiring him to use it even more savagely.

## DEFINE IT!

**blasphemy** – words that will offend God

**Court (royal)** – the place where a monarch (mainly) rules

**demerits** – opposite of good points

**dispute** – bear, 'take it'

**naught** – nothing

**vow** – promise

**whetstone** – stone used to sharpen blades

**bounty** – generosity

**fortitude** – strength to face pain or problems

**lowliness** – being humble

**perseverance** – ability to carry on in the face of difficulties

**stableness** – being rational and even-tempered

**temperance** – self-restraint; not getting drunk

**verity** – being truthful

### AQA exam-style question

Starting with this conversation, explore how Shakespeare presents the idea of manliness in *Macbeth*.

Write about:

- how Shakespeare presents the idea of manliness in this conversation
- how Shakespeare presents the idea of manliness in the play as a whole.

[30 marks]

Use the guidance on pages 84–87 to help you plan your answer.

# Character and theme essentials

## Macbeth

Macbeth meets the witches and demands to know the truth – no matter what the consequences are. His determination and willingness to face up to truth is almost admirable. However, his strong will – his struggle for absolute power – has turned him into a tyrant. The Macbeths may have cleverly framed Malcolm and Donalbain for the murder of their father, but the style of Macbeth's rule quickly makes their guilt obvious.

## Ross

Shakespeare presents Ross as a good, humble and selfless man. In Act 4 he visits Lady Macduff and offers her comfort and kindness when she feels abandoned (and is about to be murdered). Ross then has the unpleasant task of giving Macduff the news of his family's slaughter.

## Lady Macduff

This is Lady Macduff's only appearance in the play, yet she is fully created by Shakespeare: we learn enough about her to make her believable. She comes across as strong and dignified, and as a loving mother. Shakespeare seems to deliberately present her as a contrast with the warped, evil model of femininity represented by Lady Macbeth.

## Macduff

Macduff is fiercely loyal to his country and its rightful king. He is honest and brave, but he also has tender feelings: his children are 'pretty ones' and 'my pretty chickens' and he *feels* their murder 'as a man'. Shakespeare presents Macduff as a more commendable model of manliness than Macbeth.

## Witchcraft and chaos

Evil and witchcraft trigger an alarming breakdown in the natural world: the use of the witches' powers threatens disasters such as 'untie the winds' and 'swallow navigation [ships]' with 'yesty waves' (Scene 1).

## Kingship

Malcolm lists all the essential 'king-becoming graces', including 'justice, verity, temperance', and so on. There is such dignity and precision to these listed virtues that an audience is bound to take them as Shakespeare's own beliefs. They come across as a sort of manifesto for good kingship.

Kings were thought to be chosen by God, and therefore had a 'divine right' to rule. Macduff calls Duncan 'a most sainted king'. The short part of Scene 3 where we learn about King Edward's healing powers and 'sanctity' is completely unnecessary to the plot of *Macbeth*. Shakespeare seems only to have included it to emphasise the importance of saintly virtue in kings.

## Manliness

Macduff's reaction to his family's slaughter gives us a new and better model of manliness: both tears *and* determination to get justice and revenge.

## Trust and loyalty

Macduff and Ross are 'goodies': they are models of loyalty and steadfastness – sticking to what is right, rather than pursuing self-interest. These virtues have been under pressure in Ross and he regrets that in a Scotland of fear and suspicion it is hard to 'know ourselves' (Scene 2) – to stick to what we know to be right. Because of these pressures – 'the fits o' the season' - he forgives Macduff for taking the risk of leaving his family unguarded. Lady Macduff condemns her husband for this, but she doesn't know what we know. Perhaps, too, Macduff puts loyalty to his country above loyalty to his family.

**REVIEW IT!**

1  One witch says, 'something wicked this way comes'. What is the wicked thing?

2  What does Macbeth call the witches as he arrives?

3  What happens when Macbeth asks the First Apparition for 'one word more'?

4  According to the Third Apparition, what must happen before Macbeth can be beaten? (Scene 1)

5  What is reflected in the mirror carried by the eighth king?

6  When the witches disappear and Macbeth is left on his own, what does he decide to do?

7  Of what does Lady Macduff accuse her husband?

8  How does Ross try to comfort Lady Macduff?

9  Why does Lady Macduff's son say that all swearers and liars must be fools?

10  Who arrives and speaks to Lady Macduff just before the murderers arrive?

11  Why is Malcolm reluctant to help Macduff fight against Macbeth? (Scene 3)

12  Which two vices does Malcolm claim to be full of?

13  What illness is the English king, Edward the Confessor, believed to be able to cure?

14  Briefly sum up Ross's view of the condition Scotland has fallen into.

15  How does Malcolm react when Ross tells Macduff that his family has been slaughtered?

16  How might the audience react to Macbeth's final speech in Scene 1?

17  What impression do we get of Lady Macduff in Scene 2?

18  Who do you think the Messenger is in Scene 2? Who might have sent him?

19  Read Malcolm's speech in Scene 3 ('Macduff, this noble passion,...to command'). What does this speech suggest about ideal kingship?

20  At the very end of Act 4 Malcolm comforts Macduff with the words, 'The night is long that never finds the day.' What does he mean, and why are these words so fitting at this point in the play?

# Act 5

## Summary: 'Out, damned spot! Out, I say!'

Lady Macbeth's servant has asked a doctor to join her in observing Lady Macbeth's sleepwalking. Lady Macbeth arrives asleep, carrying a light. (She insists on having 'light by her continually'. She is afraid of the dark which is always linked in *Macbeth* to fear, evil and horror.)

Lady Macbeth keeps rubbing her hands and talking in a confused way as though she is reliving the killing of Duncan and the destruction of the evidence. She assures Macbeth that they have nothing to fear but then she shows her distress at Duncan's bloodshed. She keeps trying to wash her hands, and wishes that there was a perfume that could 'sweeten this little hand'. ('…will these hands ne'er be clean?' she asks. She is no longer afraid of being caught; now she is afraid of never being able to get rid of her guilt.)

The Doctor is very disturbed by what he has seen and heard, and says that Lady Macbeth probably needs a priest more than a doctor. (The Doctor concludes that Lady Macbeth is troubled by sin and guilt, not an illness, so he can do little for her.)

The Doctor tells the servant to look after Lady Macbeth and keep any means of suicide out of her reach.

## Context

Read what one student wrote about their reactions to Lady Macbeth at this point in the play. Notice how this student has put forward their own personal view of Lady Macbeth – a view that is informed by their own life experience in the 21st century. Notice also that their personal view is backed up by evidence and explanation.

> I was shocked when Lady Macbeth asked spirits to 'unsex me here'. She seemed determined to get rid of all her femininity and become 'fiend-like' - cruel, putting personal ambition above everyone else. However, when she is sleepwalking I begin to feel sympathy for her. I realise the terrible pressure this 'unsexing' has put on her. It has left her with nothing; Macbeth - the 'real' man - has as good as abandoned her while she is being driven mad by a guilt that she is suffering for him.

## Extract 1

All the repetitions match the disorder of her mind.

**LADY MACBETH**
To bed, to bed; there's knocking at the gate. Come, come, come, come, give me your hand; What's done cannot be undone. To bed, to bed, to bed.

She is still trying to control and calm Macbeth.

## Extract 2

**DOCTOR**
Foul whisp'erings are abroad. Unnatural deeds
Do breed unnatural troubles; infected minds
To their deaf pillows will discharge their secrets.
More needs she the divine than the physician.
5 God, God, forgive us all. Look after her;
Remove from her the means of all annoyance,
And still keep eyes upon her. So, good night,
My mind she has mated, and amazed my sight.

Once again, the Macbeths' crime is presented as a sin.

This expression of mental illness makes it sound physical, as though Lady Macbeth's guilt is literally destroying her brain.

The final rhyming couplet gives the Doctor's words finality, as though he is trying to regain control of himself after his shock and amazement.

# DOIT!

1 Look back through the play and find three examples of mental states being presented in terms of illness or physical pain.

2 Briefly explain the effect of these references. An example is given below. Explore two more examples.

When Lady Macbeth hears of the witches' predictions, she fears that although Macbeth is ambitious enough to make the predictions come true, his ambition lacks 'the illness should attend it.' Ambition is a mental state. Illness here is therefore mental. She seems to be hinting at the extreme, reckless actions Macbeth should take, and also the mental torment he needs to be prepared to suffer when he has succeeded. The word 'illness' is striking because you would normally assume illness to be unwelcome. Here she presents it as something desirable. The witches, too, like to turn normal expectations upside down: 'fair is foul and foul is fair', so Lady Macbeth's perverse choice of 'illness' as desirable connects her to evil too.

# DEFINEIT!

## STRETCHIT!

The Doctor's speech at the end of extract 2 above is in poetry.
The rest of the scene is not in poetry, but in prose (see page 82).

Briefly explain:

• why you think Shakespeare wrote this scene in prose, and

• why he wrote the Doctor's final speech in poetry.

**abroad** – around the area (here Scotland or the area around Macbeth's castle)

**discharge** – give away

**the divine** – God

**mated** – astonished, amazed

**physician** – doctor

## Act 5 Scene 2

### Summary: 'Those he commands move only in command'

A group of Scottish lords has turned against Macbeth and plans to join the English army at Birnam Wood. Angus reports that no one is standing by Macbeth unless he forces them to. (Caithness presents the invading armies as a sort of medicine that will 'purge' the country and restore it to health.)

## Act 5 Scene 3

### Summary: 'I'll fight, 'til from my bones my flesh be hack'd'

Increasingly isolated, Macbeth is preparing to defend his castle. His behaviour seems erratic. He hears that 10,000 soldiers are approaching but vows to fight on. He asks the Doctor to cure his wife's troubled mind, but the Doctor tells him that troubled minds have to be cured by the patient. (Macbeth, too, wants his land to be purged 'to a sound and pristine health', but for him the disease is the English invasion.)

## Act 5 Scene 4

### Summary: 'Let every soldier hew him down a bough'

At Birnam Wood, Malcolm orders the soldiers to camouflage themselves with branches. Siward warns everyone that the outcome of the battle will only be clear once it takes place. The drama of this scene comes from the audience suddenly realising that the witches have fooled Macbeth. When they said he was safe until a forest approached his castle, he assumed that meant he was safe forever.

### Madness or 'valiant fury'?

At every point, Macbeth could be described as mad or brave – or both. Here at the end of the play his angry, erratic behaviour could certainly be explained by insanity or by heroic courage. Although Macbeth has become an evil tyrant, Shakespeare still presents him as a complex and intriguing character.

**STRETCH**IT!

In what ways might Shakespeare want us to sympathise with Macbeth in these scenes? Give reasons for your thoughts.

Look at some of Macbeth's words and actions in Scene 3:

1 He dismisses Malcolm as no threat.

2 He says he is happy to be deserted by his disloyal thanes.

3 He yells abuse at his servant.

4 He says he will fight 'till from my bones my flesh be hack'd'.

5 He orders the Doctor to cure Lady Macbeth of her 'troubled' mind.

6 He yells at the Doctor.

7 He orders Seyton to help put on his armour.

For each one, decide whether it is more caused by madness or by bravery. Give reasons for your choice.

## Extract 1

This metaphor – a tightening belt – conveys the oppressive nature of Macbeth's rule.

**CAITHNESS**
Great Dunsinane he strongly fortifies.
Some say he's mad; others, that lesser hate him,
Do call it valiant fury; but, for certain,
He cannot buckle his distemper'd cause
5  Within the belt of rule.

**ANGUS**
Now does he feel
His secret murders sticking on his hands,
Now minutely revolts upbraid his faith-breach;
Those he commands move only in command,
10  Nothing in love. Now does he feel his title
Hang loose about him, like a giant's robe
Upon a dwarfish thief.

**MENTEITH**
Who then shall blame
His pester'd senses to recoil and start,
15  When all that is within him does condemn
Itself for being there?

This metaphor of Macbeth's guilt sticking to his hands reminds us of Lady Macbeth's desire to wash the guilt off their hands – in Act 5 Scene 1 and in Act 2 Scene 2.

This **simile** does not just emphasise how unfit a king Macbeth is, but also that he has *stolen* the crown. Notice the clothing metaphor here. Clothing metaphors are common in the play.

Menteith suggests a conflict in Macbeth between his terrible deeds and his natural sense of morality.

## DEFINE IT!

**distemper'd** – chaotic, broken-down

**minutely** – every minute

**purge** – to cleanse or purify, often violently

**recoil** – jump back in disgust

**upbraid** – tell off

### AQA exam-style question

Starting with this extract, explore how Shakespeare presents the attitudes of other characters to Macbeth.

Write about:

- how Shakespeare presents the attitudes of other characters to Macbeth in this extract

- how Shakespeare presents the attitudes of other characters to Macbeth in the play as a whole.

[30 marks]

Use the guidance on pages 85–87 to help you plan your answer.

Here is how one student considers Shakespeare's possible attitude in their answer to this question:

Menteith's belief that Macbeth's natural morality will 'condemn' his behaviour seems naïve in this casually delivered speech. However, Shakespeare might support this view as, earlier in the play, Macbeth was in a moral dilemma over whether to kill Duncan and had to suppress his own moral objections to do it.

## Act 5 Scene 5

### Summary: 'Out, out, brief candle!'

Macbeth insists that his forces can outlast a siege of the castle. After a woman's cry has been heard, Seyton reports that Lady Macbeth is dead. The news makes Macbeth reflect on the brevity and pointlessness of life. (Macbeth's reaction to Lady Macbeth's death can be read in two ways: he hardly cares, or he wishes she had died later – at a better time.)

A messenger shocks Macbeth with news that Birnam Wood appears to be approaching. Macbeth fears that the witches told him 'lies like truth', but he remains determined to fight to the end. Macbeth learns a central lesson of the play: you can't trust appearances. The witches' predictions *seemed* to mean that he was safe forever.

## Act 5 Scene 6

### Summary: 'Make all our trumpets speak'

Malcolm orders his soldiers to remove their camouflage. He tells Siward to attack with his son. Malcolm and Macduff will follow up the attack. (Increasingly Malcolm is taking on the role of military commander.)

## Act 5 Scene 7

### Summary: 'Swords I smile at, weapons laugh to scorn'

Young Siward finds Macbeth, but Macbeth kills him and observes, 'Thou wast born of woman.' Macduff is closing in on Macbeth and vows to fight no one except Macbeth. Siward tells Malcolm that Macbeth's army surrendered without a fight, and he invites Malcolm into the castle.

### Structure and context

These final scenes in Act 5 are short and fast moving, cutting from place to place. They work very well in films: modern cinema audiences are used to quick switches from one location to another. To make these quick location changes work on Shakespeare's stage would have been challenging though, especially given the huge scale of the action, with whole armies moving between woods, hills and a castle.

Shakespeare's plays were normally performed in an open-air theatre, but it seems *Macbeth* (one of the later plays) was first performed at Hampton Court Palace in front of King James I and his guest, King Christian of Denmark. Probably it was performed indoors. This might have made the final scenes even harder to portray, but on the other hand, it would have allowed the performance to be under artificial lights, which might have made the atmosphere of darkness that runs through much of the play more effective.

## Extract 1

> Macbeth starts with a 'brief candle' as a metaphor for life.

> Finally, Macbeth explores a new metaphor – life as 'a tale told by an idiot'.

**MACBETH**
Out, out, brief candle!
Life's but a walking shadow, a poor player
That struts and frets his hour upon the stage
And then is heard no more. It is a tale
5 Told by an idiot, full of sound and fury,
Signifying nothing.

> His metaphor then changes as he develops an image of life as an actor who lasts only a very short time on the stage of life.

## Metaphors of life

All three of Macbeth's metaphors of life are rich in meanings and **connotations**. Here is how one student wrote about the first one:

The choice of a 'brief candle' as a symbol of life fits Macbeth's experience of life during the play. A candle gives light, and light is associated with hope, but the light from a candle is dim, does not stretch far and is vulnerable to being snuffed out. Macbeth now understands just how weak his own position is - and always has been: he is the 'brief candle'. His words 'out, out' are a sad recognition of this simple truth - a truth he has tried to hide from himself ever since he was excited by the witches' predictions.

**DO IT!**

Analyse the other two metaphors Macbeth uses in extract 1. Explore their meaning and their effect.

| Metaphor | Analysis |
| --- | --- |
| A poor player | |
| A tale told by an idiot | |

## DEFINE IT!

**fret** – shout or perform noisily

**scorn** - contempt

**signifying** – meaning

**strut** – walk in a proud and showy way

### Extract 2

An actor would have to interpret Macbeth's feelings here. Macbeth is still determined to fight on, and he believes that he is still magically protected.

> **MACBETH**
> Thou wast born of woman.
> But swords I smile at, weapons laugh to scorn,
> Brandish'd by man that's of a woman born.

The rhyming couplet ('scorn'/'born') reinforces Macbeth's confidence – or is it just empty bravado?

## Act 5 Scene 8

## Summary: 'Macduff was from his mother's womb untimely ripp'd'

Macduff finds and fights Macbeth. Macbeth tells Macduff he cannot be beaten by 'one of woman born'. Macduff replies that he was not 'born': he was cut from his mother's womb. (Macduff's description of his birth – 'from his mother's womb/Untimely ripp'd' might suggest that his 'birth' was a by-product of his mother's brutal murder?)

Disheartened, Macbeth condemns the witches' deception – their use of words with 'a double sense'. He says he won't fight Macduff, but Macduff threatens to put Macbeth on public display like a fairground monster. (Macduff wants to humiliate Macbeth to avenge the slaughter of his family.)

This humiliation is too much for Macbeth, so he resumes his fight.

## DO IT!

What are Macbeth's feelings at this point? Is he callous and cruel? Contemptuous? You decide.

Imagine you are directing the play. Give some advice to an actor about how you want them to interpret Macbeth at this point. Explain your advice.

Start your advice with these words: *I want you to imagine that at this point in the play Macbeth is…*Continue to give and explain your advice about Macbeth's feelings at this point. You could give the actor advice about techniques such as gesture and tone.

## Act 5 Scene 9

### Summary: 'Hail, King of Scotland!'

Ross informs Old Siward of his son's death in battle. Old Siward is glad he died as 'God's soldier'. (Old Siward rejects Malcolm's offer of 'more sorrow' for his son's death. For Old Siward it is enough that his son died honourably and has earned God's blessing.)

Macduff arrives with Macbeth's head and everyone hails Malcolm as King of Scotland.

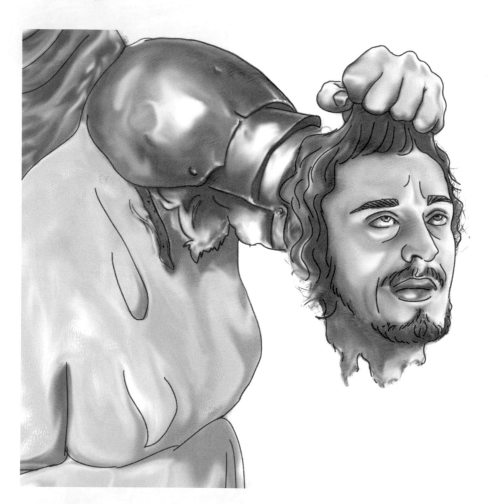

Malcolm thanks his thanes and promotes them all to earls. He announces his intention of calling home those who have fled Scotland for their safety. He mentions that Lady Macbeth is believed to have committed suicide. He invites everyone to his coronation. (Malcolm calls Macbeth 'this dead butcher' and Lady Macbeth 'fiend-like'.)

### Macbeth, the 'butcher'

Malcolm's judgement of Macbeth as a 'butcher' is **hyperbole**, but Macbeth's killings are coldly savage. At the beginning of the play, the Captain's description of Macbeth in battle hints at actual butchery: to get to the traitor Macdonald, Macbeth 'carved out his passage' and 'unseam'd him from the nave to the chaps' as though he is neatly dividing Macdonald's body into parcels of meat.

**DO IT!**

In Act 5 Scene 3, Macbeth promises to 'fight till from my bones my flesh be hack'd'.

Explain how in these words Shakespeare prepares us for Malcolm's description of Macbeth as 'this dead butcher'.

## Extract 1

> **ROSS**
> Your son, my lord, has paid a soldier's debt.
> He only lived but till he was a man,
> The which no sooner had his prowess confirm'd
> In the unshrinking station where he fought,
> 5 But like a man he died.
>
> **SIWARD**
> Then he is dead?
>
> **ROSS**
> Ay, and brought off the field. Your cause of sorrow
> Must not be measured by his worth, for then
> It hath no end.
>
> **SIWARD**
> 10 Had he his hurts before?
>
> **ROSS**
> Ay, on the front.
>
> **SIWARD**
> Why then, God's soldier be he!
> Had I as many sons as I have hairs,
> I would not wish them to a fairer death.
> 15 And so his knell is knoll'd.

**Siward's son became a complete man by behaving in a 'manly' way in battle.**

**Ross expects Siward to suffer sorrow.**

**Yet Siward is mainly interested in *how* his son died. His wounds are in his front ('before') and therefore he got them fighting, not running away.**

**Ross points out that any soldier knows he risks dying.**

**Siward takes the news stoically.**

**Siward seems to simply accept his son's death: he couldn't hope for a better ('fairer') death for any son.**

### DEFINE IT!

**knell** – funeral bell

**knolled** – rung

**prowess** – great ability

**station** – position

**stoically** – accepting hardship without complaining

**unshrinking** – unflinching, never showing any fear

## Death and grief

In Shakespeare's time (17th century) and more so in Macbeth's (medieval times), death often arrived suddenly and often painfully. Perhaps Siward is just being realistic when he accepts death so uncomplainingly.

### AQA exam-style question

Starting with this extract, explore how Shakespeare presents soldiers and war in *Macbeth*.

Write about:

- how Shakespeare presents soldiers and war in this extract

- how Shakespeare presents soldiers and war in the play as a whole.

[30 marks]

Use the guidance on pages 84–87 to help you plan your answer.

Study the question carefully and annotate it as necessary. Make some brief notes for each paragraph of your answer. Refer to about three other points in the play which deal with soldiers/war. Plan to comment on the effects of a few brief, relevant quotations. Plan to refer to relevant, useful aspects of context.

# Character and theme essentials

## Lady Macbeth

Watching Lady Macbeth sleepwalking and desperately trying to clean the guilt from her hands, the Doctor concludes that 'More needs she the divine than the physician.' He suggests that her illness is not a physical one, not even just a mental one: instead her mind has been 'infected' by guilt. Cure depends on confessing her sins. Shakespeare shows us Lady Macbeth through the eyes of the Doctor and the Gentlewoman who both express pity for her. 'I would not have such a heart,' says the Gentlewoman, and the Doctor notes that 'The heart is sorely charged'. This compassion they both express for her now makes her appear more pitiful than evil.

## Macbeth

Macbeth refuses to be defeated by the approaching armies or by his conscience. He has moments of thoughtful regret – about the curses he has earned, and about his wife's death – but mostly he is full of violent defiance. His defence is hopeless because his army hates him, and because the witches have given him false assurances of his invincibility. Yet he bravely fights to the end – even when he knows that death is almost certain.

## Malcolm

Malcolm grows into a leader, commanding his men in battle, and accepting the crown with dignity and confidence: his final speech is like a manifesto for the first days of his rule, delivered as though it has been carefully planned.

## Macduff

Macduff is single-minded in his pursuit of Macbeth. He refuses to waste his fighting skills and his energy on anyone else. He insists on fighting Macbeth face on, not killing him from behind when he has the opportunity. (He tells Macbeth to 'turn'.) Macduff is savage in his revenge but he sticks to the rules of combat, giving Macbeth the chance to defend himself. He is the 'king maker', the killer of the 'thief' king Macbeth and the first person to hail Malcolm as king.

## Guilt and mental torment

Lady Macbeth has a 'mind diseased' by guilt, fear and – probably – a sense of abandonment by Macbeth. Macbeth's own behaviour is crazed and full of abuse and random unkindness towards his servants, but his own mental torment seems to be calming. His violence has brought him a 'direness familiar': he is so used to horrors that they no longer weaken him.

## Kingship and leadership

There are two opposing models of kingship on display in Act 5: Macbeth's tyranny that involves unpredictable decisions, and threats. His authority comes from intimidation and bribery, so that his only soldiers are those '*hired* to bear their staves' (Macduff, Scene 7). Malcolm's authority comes from his ability to lead and motivate his men, and to sympathise with their losses. He promises Siward that his dead soldier son is 'worth more sorrow'.

## Manliness and duty

Siward is satisfied with Ross's report that his son died 'like a man' and that in dying he 'paid his score' (carried out his duty). Siward's response to his son's death suggests that duty to king and country is even more important than duty to family.

**REVIEW IT!**

1 Who brings a doctor to watch Lady Macbeth's sleepwalking?

2 What information does the Gentlewoman give about Lady Macbeth's hand rubbing?

3 What two pieces of advice does the Doctor give the Gentlewoman?

4 How does Lennox know that Donalbain is not with the invading army?

5 How do we know that no one is willingly supporting Macbeth?

6 For what two reasons is Macbeth not afraid of defeat?

7 Why can't Macbeth look forward to old age?

8 Why does Macbeth say he will have nothing to do with medicine? ('I'll none of it.')

9 What does Malcolm order his soldiers to do, and why?

10 How did Lady Macbeth die?

11 What does the Messenger report seeing to Macbeth?

12 How and why does Malcolm decide to attack Macbeth's castle?

13 What is Macbeth's 'lie' that Young Siward wants to prove wrong?

14 Why does Macduff hope that Macbeth is still alive?

15 In your own words, explain what Macduff will do with Macbeth if he surrenders.

16 Why does Siward reject offers of sorrow for his dead son?

17 Malcolm announces his intention of 'producing forth the cruel ministers' of the Macbeths. Explain what he might mean by this.

18 Macbeth says that he is no longer startled by frightening thoughts and sights. Explain what this shows about how he has changed during the play.

19 At the beginning of Scene 7 Macbeth says, 'They have tied me to a stake; I cannot fly,/But bear-like I must fight the course.' Explain what these words reveal about what Macbeth is thinking and feeling at this point.

20 Act 5 ends with the defeat and killing of Macbeth and with the rightful king about to be crowned. Do you think the play ends optimistically? Give reasons for your views.

# Characters

## Macbeth

### What we know about Macbeth

- He is married to Lady Macbeth.
- He is a commander of the Scottish army.
- He is a nobleman, the Thane of Glamis.
- King Duncan rewards him with the title of Thane of Cawdor.
- He meets three witches who predict that he will become king.
- Lady Macbeth persuades him to kill King Duncan.
- He murders anyone he considers a threat to his position.
- He is defeated and killed by Macduff.

### Macbeth the hero

At the start of the play, Macbeth is presented as a hero who risks his own life for the sake of Scotland and King Duncan. The wounded Captain gives a glowing account of the heroic actions of 'brave Macbeth'. Ross's report suggests Macbeth is so at home in battle that he is 'Bellona's bridegroom' – a metaphor that presents him as the new husband of the goddess of war.

Here are two students writing about their impressions of Macbeth in Act 1:

> ### Student answer A
>
> Our first impression of Macbeth is that he is a hero who has saved his king and his country: in the battle Macbeth was 'disdaining fortune', the Captain tells Duncan. This shows that he ignored the risk to his own life – the fate threatening every soldier. 'Brave Macbeth' focuses entirely on killing Macdonald who is a traitor to Scotland.

> ### Student answer B
>
> The Captain's description of Macbeth's way of fighting is over the top. Macbeth seems to relish violence and the physical hacking into flesh: Macbeth 'carv'd out his passage' to Macdonald, and when he reached Macdonald he 'unseam'd him'. Shakespeare seems to be suggesting that Macbeth isn't just fighting efficiently and bravely, he's loving it! His cruel savagery is disturbing. Of course, perhaps the Captain is exaggerating.

**Evidence**

Notice how these students use evidence to support their views. They use two sorts of evidence: they refer to parts of the play, and they quote relevant words. Both students build quotations naturally into their own sentences.

# Evil Macbeth

Does Shakespeare want us to see Macbeth as naturally evil, or as a brave hero who *becomes* evil? The witches seem to have power over Macbeth. His very first words, just before he meets the witches, are, 'So foul and fair a day I have not seen' (Act 1 Scene 3) and these words echo the witches' own words in Scene 1. Is Shakespeare using this repetition to signal to us that Macbeth is in the witches' power?

By Act 3 the witches seem to be speaking directly through Macbeth. His speeches at the end of Scene 2, when he is hinting to his wife that he has planned 'a deed of dreadful note' – Banquo's murder – contain long sentences filled with the imagery of witchcraft that sound like the end of a spell.

Look at this list of words that *might* be appropriate to Macbeth:

**unwise   deceived   romantic   clever   reckless   brave   self-pitying   heroic   evil**

Think carefully about these nine words and put them into a rank order from the most to the least true. You might find that the top half of your rank order contains both negative and positive words.

Find evidence to support your top three word choices.

# Macbeth the tyrant?

The first time Macbeth is called a tyrant is by Lennox in Act 3 Scene 6. From that point on, Macbeth is referred to as 'the tyrant' over and over again. Macduff looks forward to freeing Scotland from 'the tyrant's grasp' (Act 4 Scene 3). The word 'grasp' suggests a tight but desperate hold. Ross says that Macbeth's oppressive rule has turned Scotland into 'a grave'.

# How do *we* feel about Macbeth?

Surely everyone will be appalled by Macbeth, yet he does have some virtues: he is brave and selfless in battle, he has a conscience (at first) and he is a loving husband (at first). Of course, how we feel depends on who 'we' are. Perhaps Shakespeare's own audience would readily believe in the existence of witches and their ability to corrupt a good man. After all, their own king, James I, had written a book about witchcraft and believed that Scottish witches were plotting to kill him.

**STRETCH IT!**

Might a modern and Shakespearean audience come up with different rank orders? Explain your thoughts.

# Lady Macbeth

## What we know about Lady Macbeth

- She is married to Macbeth.

- She persuades him to murder King Duncan and comes up with the perfect murder plan.

- After Macbeth has carried out the murder, she goes to the murder scene and plants the murder weapons on Duncan's guards as false evidence.

- She has had at least one baby, but she seems no longer to have any children.

- She sleepwalks, probably disturbed by her guilt.

- She dies – almost certainly by suicide.

## Lady Macbeth the schemer

Lady Macbeth leaves nothing to chance: she plans the murder of Duncan carefully so that someone else will be blamed for it. She gets Duncan's guards drunk so that they will be unable to defend Duncan or to defend themselves against the planting of false evidence. Her plans depend on deception: she deceives the thanes about the guards' guilt, but she also puts on a show of loyalty and hospitality to Duncan that will make it unthinkable that she could ever want to harm him. When Duncan's body is discovered she convincingly acts as if she is shocked.

## Lady Macbeth the witch?

Malcolm finally calls her 'fiend-like', and her evil is suggested not just in her actions but also in the language Shakespeare gives her. For example, she doesn't just tell Macbeth that she would always keep promises, but she would even have 'dash'd the brains out' of her own baby if she had promised to kill it (Act 1 Scene 7). Her choice of language is brutal and graphic, suggesting she would not just kill her own baby, but enjoy it. In her speech in Act 1 Scene 5 just before Macbeth arrives, she actively summons 'spirits' to strengthen her in the evil she will need to kill Duncan. Her repeated call, 'Come...', creates a hypnotic, spell-like atmosphere around her words.

## Lady Macbeth the man?

Lady Macbeth knows that she must *appear* womanly, yet 'unsex' herself – become 'manly' – to gain the strength to commit murder. Macbeth admires the traditionally manly qualities that his wife finds in herself. 'Bring forth men-children only', he responds admiringly to the brilliant daring of her murder plan. He is impressed by her manly 'undaunted mettle' (Act 1 Scene 7). However, her sleep-walking in Act 5 Scene 1 shows the Doctor that her 'heart is sorely charged': she has only *suppressed* her gentle side, and it is reclaiming her.

# How should we feel about Lady Macbeth?

We are probably appalled and fascinated by Lady Macbeth's evil scheming and her manipulation of Macbeth. However, by the end of the play we might see her more as a victim, used and abandoned by Macbeth. Her guilt-driven sleep-walking might evoke pity in an audience. Modern audiences often sympathise with Lady Macbeth as a strong woman in a male-dominated society who feels frustrated by the limits on her ambition. Perhaps, too, grief at the loss of her children and her father have hardened her.

Here are some words which *might* be used about Lady Macbeth:

**devious   independent   unhappy   loving   brave   desperate   evil   manly**

Choose the two words from the list above that you think are *most* true of Lady Macbeth.

Explain your choices with reference to language and events in the text.

Does your choice differ at different points in the play?

# Writing about Lady Macbeth

Read part of what one student wrote about Lady Macbeth. Notice how the student uses evidence to support their points:

I don't know how I feel about Lady Macbeth. I know she's driven mad and finally kills herself because of her guilt, but I can't forget her evil cunning at the start of the play. She wants to 'unsex' her womanliness and become completely evil, and she seems excited by this idea. We know she is excited because she asks evil spirits to 'come to my woman's breasts and take my milk for gall' and to 'pall thee in the dunnest smoke of hell'. She just seems so enthusiastic about it all! Macbeth's only just got home from some serious slaughtering and she's assuming he wants to get on and kill the king and she's got it all so worked out that he can 'leave all the rest to' her. There's nothing innocent about her at all: she's greedy and scheming and she gets what's coming to her.

**STRETCH IT!**

What other words could be used to sum up Lady Macbeth? Choose two words not on the list above and explain why they are particularly true of Lady Macbeth.

Look at the mark scheme on page 86. Give special attention to the criteria for choosing and using evidence (AO1) and commenting on the effects of language choices (AO2).

What are the strengths of the student's answer? Give the student some brief advice about how to improve their answer.

**NAIL IT!**

In your AQA exam, when you write about a character, make sure you make clear points in answer to the question and back up your points by referring to events and language in the play.

# Other important characters

## Duncan

A recent production of the play suggested that Macbeth's main motive for killing Duncan was that he considered Duncan's weaknesses a threat to the country that Macbeth had risked his own life to save. Some actors have portrayed Duncan as weak and dithery. Others have portrayed him as powerful and decisive, sometimes even uncaring about the sufferings of his soldiers.

Although Duncan is amazed at how inaccurately he judged Cawdor, he doesn't seem to have learnt any lessons from this: he continues to trust appearances. So when he arrives at Macbeth's castle where Lady Macbeth has decided to kill him before morning, he decides that the castle has 'a pleasant seat' and immediately drops his guard. It is not clear what Shakespeare wants us to think of Duncan.

## Banquo

Shakespeare's king, James I, was also King of Scotland, and a descendant of Banquo. James was therefore at the end of the line of kings the witches promised would descend from Banquo. Since James was also the patron and protector of Shakespeare's theatre company, it was important to show Banquo as a good man who resists temptation to achieve his ambitions through force. He insists to Macbeth that he is willing to talk about the witches' predictions as he can keep his 'bosom franchised and allegiance clear'. In other words, he will do nothing to fulfil the witches' predictions that clashes with his loyalty to Duncan or commits him to immoral acts.

## Macduff

Like Banquo, Macduff is honest and puts the interests of his country above his personal interests. In that respect, Shakespeare presents him as the opposite of what Macbeth becomes. Macduff finds Duncan's body and is deeply shocked ('O horror, horror, horror'). His shock reflects his loyalty to the king. He tracks down and kills Macbeth not just in personal revenge but also because Macbeth is a tyrant who has destroyed Macduff's beloved country, Scotland.

## Malcolm

Malcolm and his brother Donalbain run away when Duncan – their father – is murdered. They suspect that they will be next. In exile Malcolm is cautious about who he trusts: he knows that Macbeth will try to trap and murder him. By the end of the play, though, he has become openly confident, boosting his men's morale and leading them into battle. Hailed as the new king, he immediately delivers a speech that sounds pre-rehearsed and majestic. He sounds bold and decisive like Macbeth, yet sensitive like his father. We don't know how Shakespeare would have presented him in a sequel to Macbeth but here he seems like the king that Scotland deserves.

# Different interpretations of characters

It is important to remember that how an actor decides to play a character will greatly influence how we, the audience, respond to that character. For example, some actors have played Lady Macbeth sympathetically; others have played her as a cruel witch. Actors do not convey these different interpretations by altering Shakespeare's words; they convey them through gesture, movement and voice expression. Of course, as you read the play to yourself, you too will be bringing your own interpretations to characters.

**NAILIT!**

In your AQA exam, keep an open mind. Think about different ways characters can be interpreted, or presented by actors. Use tentative words such as 'perhaps', 'might', 'could be' to help you consider more than one view of a character or theme.

## REVIEW IT!

1  Who describes 'his brandish'd steel,/Which smoked with bloody execution', and who is he referring to?

2  How is this description typical of that character's battle report?

3  Who says, 'What he hath lost, noble Macbeth hath won', and about who?

4  How is the speaker showing his gratitude?

5  Who says, 'look like the innocent flower,/But be the serpent under it' and to whom is it said?

6  What does this show about the speaker?

7  Who says, 'Whiles I threat, he lives;/Words to the heat of deeds too cold breath gives.' and about who?

8  How is this thought typical of the speaker?

9  Who says, 'The repetition in a woman's ear/Would murder as it fell', and to who?

10  Why does the speaker say this?

11  Who says, 'We have scotch'd the snake, not kill'd it'?

12  What does the speaker mean?

13  Who says, 'Then live, Macduff. What need I fear thee'?

14  Why does the speaker say this?

15  Macduff calls Macbeth a 'tyrant' (Act 4 Scene 3). Write down at least three other things that Macbeth is called.

16  Why does Malcolm tell Macduff that Macbeth will 'seem as pure as snow' compared to him (Malcolm) (Act 4 Scene 3)?

17  What could be considered Macbeth's greatest faults?

18  Explain at least one criticism that Lady Macbeth expresses about Macbeth.

19  Choose *one* of these characters: Macbeth, Lady Macbeth, the witches. Explain how your chosen character could be seen sympathetically by the audience. You could consider how an actor might play the character to make them more sympathetic.

20  Explain which character – other than Macbeth or Lady Macbeth – could be seen as the most important character in the play. Justify your choice.

# Themes and contexts

## Power and kingship

King James VI of Scotland became King James I of England

In Shakespeare's England, kings were seen as chosen by God and therefore had a 'divine right' to rule. All power was in their hands. In reality, of course, a king who ignored all advice and ruled in his own and not his people's interests could expect to be overthrown. Kings therefore had to be cautious, merciful and sensitive to their people's needs and wishes. Even Macbeth – a perfect example of a tyrant – has to *appear* to stick to the law. He dare not be *seen* to 'sweep' Banquo away 'with barefaced power' (Act 3 Scene 1).

As king of Scotland, James I had already shown a taste for 'barefaced power'. In *Macbeth,* Shakespeare shows the importance of using power responsibly through good kingship. James I was Shakespeare's patron and it seems likely that either Shakespeare was hoping to influence James or flatter him.

*Macbeth* showcases three examples of virtuous kingship: the 'sainted' King Duncan; King Edward the holy healer; King Malcolm, the firm and just leader. Macbeth is the opposite of all these: all power and no justice. His 'achievement' was what Malcolm pretended his own kingship would involve – to:

> " Pour the sweet milk of concord into hell,
> Uproar the universal peace, confound
> All unity on earth.' (Act 4 Scene 3) "

Malcolm and Macduff discuss the essential conditions of good kingship, but those conditions are summed up in Malcolm's words above: concord (agreement), peace and unity between the citizens (and ruler). A typical AQA exam-style question about power and kingship might be:

Annotate the question (see page 84) and analyse it (see page 85) in preparation for writing an answer.

### AQA exam-style questions

- *[Starting with this extract,]* explore how Shakespeare presents power and kingship in *Macbeth.*

- *[Starting with this conversation,]* explore how far Shakespeare presents Malcolm as an ideal model of kingship in *Macbeth.*

Use the guidance on pages 84–87 to help you plan your answer.

# Ambition

Ambition is usually seen as a good thing, and the Macbeths are certainly ambitious. However, their ambition is entirely selfish, and they will do anything to achieve it. This single-minded pursuit of ambition is what Lady Macbeth means by 'the illness' that must go with it (Act 1 Scene 5). The self-destructive nature of this sort of ambition makes Macbeth hesitate to kill Duncan: he fears that he is in the grip of 'Vaulting ambition, which o'erleaps itself/And falls on the other' (Act 1 Scene 7). Shakespeare's positive version of ambition is embodied by Macduff, Siward and Malcolm, who are all more ambitious for the health of their country than for themselves and their own family.

# Trust and loyalty

Duncan's 'absolute trust' in the Thane of Cawdor might suggest that Duncan is a fatally poor judge of character, but the reality was that kings had to trust some people. Trust by a ruler and loyalty from his subjects depended on each other. We see this principle working in reverse for Macbeth: he trusts no one and is eventually abandoned by everyone except those who give him only insincere 'mouth-honour' (Act 5 Scene 3).

To be trusted by the king was an honour to be cherished. Macbeth knows this, and wanting to 'wear' Duncan's trust and honours 'now in their newest gloss' rather than 'casting them aside' (Act 1 Scene 7) is another reason why he decides not to kill Duncan. Of course, his metaphor, 'gloss' (a mere surface shine), might suggest that Macbeth's sense of honour is shallow.

## Writing about trust in *Macbeth*

See how one student tries to establish a clear and original point about the role of trust in *Macbeth*. An examiner has made some notes alongside.

| | |
|---|---|
| Macbeth's most destructive effect on Scotland is to undermine trust. His spies and stealthy murderers are everywhere so that no one dares to trust anyone else. Malcolm cannot even trust Macduff and has to perform an elaborate test of his loyalty. The Lord tells Lennox that he yearns to be able to 'Do faithful homage, and receive free honours' once again. Life has become unbearable without honesty and openness. Yet, ironically, it is Macbeth's trust of the witches that accelerates his downfall. | Clear and plausible point of view.<br><br>Examples strengthen the opening statement.<br><br>Practical effects of the breakdown of trust are identified.<br><br>Interesting angle: even Macbeth relies on trust in some circumstances. |

**STRETCH IT!**

Read Lady Macbeth's 'ambition' speech in Act 1 Scene 5 (from 'Glamis thou art' to 'crown'd withal.')

Explain how Shakespeare's language in this speech presents Lady Macbeth's ambition negatively.

**DO IT!**

Find other examples of trust or loyalty in the play. Here are two to get you started:

Macbeth's reason for not killing Duncan: 'He's here in double trust:' (Act 1 Scene 7)

Macbeth's view of the witches after he has met them for the second time: '...damn'd all those that trust them!' (Act 4 Scene 1)

Find at least two other examples of the language of evil and the supernatural in *Macbeth*.

Explain how the language in these examples affects the audience (or reader).

# Evil and the supernatural

A play that features witches gloating over the miseries they inflict on humans while they stir up potions and spells is bound to have an atmosphere of evil. For example, while Duncan was being murdered, Lennox heard 'lamentings…i' the air' and 'strange screams of death' (Act 2 Scene 3). More of these typical horror ingredients dominate Macbeth's spell-like description of the coming of night, including 'the crow makes wing to the rooky wood' and the rousing of 'night's black agents' (Act 3 Scene 2).

## King James I

Perhaps it is significant that King James, Shakespeare's king, believed that witches and evil were active forces in the world, luring people into wicked plots and deeds – especially against James himself. Perhaps the richly evil atmosphere of *Macbeth* was meant to confirm James' superstitions while reassuring him that a good king like Malcolm (and – by implication – like James) would always overcome the forces of evil.

# Sin and guilt

Killing Duncan is a sin that Macbeth knows will lead to his 'deep damnation' – being sent to hell (Act 1 Scene 7). Once Macbeth has gone down the road of evil, there is no turning back: after being frightened by Banquo's ghost, Macbeth realises that he is 'in blood/Stepp'd in so far' that he can only carry on and secure his position with even more bloodshed (Act 3 Scene 5).

Although Banquo's ghost is an exciting theatrical device, it is mainly a projection of the guilt that is tormenting Macbeth. This guilt torment is part of the Macbeths' punishment, the implication being that they can hide their crime from the world, but not from God. This point is emphasised by the Doctor's conclusion that Lady Macbeth 'More needs…the divine than the physician.' and so she can only hope for God's forgiveness (Act 5 Scene 1).

# Nature and chaos

In Shakespeare's time, there was a traditional belief that witches' powers would cause disturbances in nature – storms, volcanoes, famine, and so on. It is these effects that Macbeth is willing to risk in exchange for the witches' predictions (Act 4 Scene 1). Natural order – including the obedience that subjects should give their king – was assumed to be God-given, and a sin as great as the killing of a king could be expected to set off a chain of terrible, 'unnatural' events. Duncan's murder is followed by events such as the blowing down of chimneys, darkness in the day and horses eating each other.

Most people today are sceptical about supposed connections between 'evil' acts, chaos in nature and the anger of a God, but in Shakespeare's day people were only too used to sudden, catastrophic events whose cause could not be explained. For example, plague kept breaking out and killing hundreds of people before disappearing again. In the absence of a rational explanation, people were more ready to blame some great evil for the catastrophe. A typical AQA exam-style question about the natural order might be:

### AQA exam-style questions

- *[Starting with this speech,]* explore how Shakespeare presents the idea of natural order in *Macbeth*.

- *[Starting with this extract,]* explore how Shakespeare presents the natural world in *Macbeth*.

Use the guidance on pages 84–87 to help you plan your answer.

**DO IT!**

Annotate the question (see page 84) and analyse it (see page 85) in preparation for writing an answer.

# Men and women

Malcolm praises Macduff when he overcomes his grief at the slaughter of his family to vow to take revenge (Act 4 Scene 3). Fighting and dying for a cause is presented as a noble thing. Siward accepts the death of his son in battle with minimal sorrow because he died 'like a man', doing his duty as a soldier (Act 5 Scene 9).

Macbeth uses accusations of unmanly cowardice to shame the murderers into killing Banquo. Lady Macbeth goads Macbeth into agreeing to kill Duncan by suggesting that his reluctance is unmanly. At first, even Macbeth speaks out against these false versions of manhood:

> " I dare do all that may become a man;
> Who dares do more is none.' (Act 1 Scene 7) "

Manliness is more than bravery. It includes tender emotions. Malcolm urges the grief-stricken Macduff to express his feelings, to 'give sorrow words', and Macduff insists that before planning revenge, he 'must also feel it like a man'.

The traditional features of 'womanliness', on the other hand, are a barrier to effective evil. Evil women have to 'unsex' themselves and turn into men. The witches have beards (Act 1 Scene 3). Lady Macbeth asks for her breasts to be filled with poison ('gall') instead of milk. Traditional assumptions about the normal features of womanhood are a helpful cover for Lady Macbeth's evil. She is so far from being suspected of Duncan's murder that the normally suspicious Macduff even shields her from hearing about it.

**DO IT!**

Choose a character who seems to have particular ideas about 'manliness'.

Briefly explain how that character uses those ideas to influence another character.

# Madness and sleep

Both Macbeth and Lady Macbeth suffer mental torment due to their guilt and through their fear of being caught. This torment is graphically expressed by Macbeth in the metaphor that his mind is 'full of scorpions' (Act 3 Scene 2). You can easily imagine the pain he is in – almost a physical pain. As soon as Macbeth kills Duncan he fears that he will 'sleep no more' (Act 2 Scene 2), and after his crazed raving at his feast, Lady Macbeth prescribes 'sleep' as the cure (Act 3 Scene 4). Of course, this cure stops working for her: by the beginning of Act 5 she is no longer sleeping peacefully but walking in her sleep, her 'slumbery agitation' being a symptom of her madness (Act 5 Scene 1).

# Appearance and reality

Once Macbeth has decided to kill Duncan, he says, 'False face must hide what the false heart doth know.' (Act 1 Scene 7) This idea of 'false face' runs right through *Macbeth*: characters put on facial expressions and play roles to fool other characters. Duncan was completely fooled by Cawdor's face, whose expressions inspired Duncan's trust. When Cawdor turns out to be a traitor, Duncan has to conclude that 'There's no art/To find the mind's construction in the face' (Act 1 Scene 4). Duncan has learned that it is impossible to read someone's mind by 'reading' their face – and not just Cawdor's: he seems to have reached a general rule about not trusting people.

Yet when Duncan arrives at Macbeth's castle, he reads the 'face' of the castle – its appearance – as a sign that he will be safe there: its 'air/ Nimbly and sweetly recommends itself/Unto our gentle senses.' His companion, Banquo, confirms this comforting impression of the castle when he observes that 'the air is delicate' (Act 1 Scene 6). In fact, Lady Macbeth has only just advised Macbeth to hide his evil intentions beneath an innocent-looking face, and she now greets Duncan with exaggerated respect. Surely Duncan – with his experience of treachery – should be wary at least.

Duncan is at least partly responsible for his own fate. Perhaps Shakespeare is saying that such gullibility in a king is inexcusable. Later, Shakespeare shows us that Duncan's son, Malcolm, has learned not to trust appearances. When Macduff asks for his support to overthrow Macbeth, Malcolm is wary. He apologises to Macduff for his suspicions but explains that he has to consider his 'own safeties' (Act 4 Scene 3).

A typical AQA exam-style question about deceptive appearances might be:

### AQA exam-style questions

*[Starting with this conversation,]* explore how Shakespeare presents the idea that appearances can be deceptive in Macbeth.

Write about:

- how Shakespeare presents deceptive appearances in this conversation
- how Shakespeare presents deceptive appearances in the play as a whole.

Use the guidance on pages 84–87 to help you plan your answer.

## DEFINE IT!

**beguile** – deceive

**conceal** – hide

**deceptive** – tending to look true when actually being false

**gullibility** – the tendency to be fooled easily

Read this paragraph from one student's answer to the question above:

> One important aspect of deceptive appearances is concealment: characters skilfully disguising their real intentions. The traitor, Thane of Cawdor, hid his real 'mind's construction' from Duncan's examination of his expressions. He must have done this very well because Duncan had 'absolute trust in him'. In fact Duncan says he 'built' that trust in Cawdor, implying that it was deep and willing on the part of Duncan. This sort of deliberate concealment is all around Duncan: Lady Macbeth's advice to her husband to 'beguile the time' - to fool people by putting on the 'right', expected expression, is easily accepted by Macbeth, as though he is perfectly used to the tactic. What is impressive about the Macbeths is that, for a while at least, they manage to fool powerful men who must be used to villains cleverly concealing their real intentions.

Useful exploration of the connotations of one word.

The paragraph ends with an original insight into what Shakespeare might be implying about concealment.

Notice how this student uses evidence. First, they make a clear point that is directly relevant to the exam question and then back up their point with textual references. Here those references are neatly built into the student's own sentences.

## NAIL IT!

When revising themes, build up a useful list of words linked to that theme.

## DO IT!

Write down at least seven more words that are relevant to the theme of the difference between appearance and reality.

Next to each word write its definition.

Here are two words to start you off: 'camouflage', 'hide'.

## NAILIT!

- A context is only relevant if it sheds light on the play and your exam question.

- Answering your exam question carefully and thoughtfully is the best way to help you consider the play's context.

- Do not write down contextual information *for its own sake* use it to support a point you are making.

# Context

Context means one or all of the following:

- ideas and influences at the time the play was written

- ideas and expectations a modern audience/reader might bring to the play

- how an extract of the play fits into the whole play.

## Using contextual information

Here are parts of two different students' answers to a question about how Shakespeare presents kingship in Macbeth. The references to context are underlined:

### Student answer A

When the eighth spirit shows reflections of one of Banquo's descendants carrying 'two-fold balls and treble sceptres', <u>you can't help feeling that Shakespeare included this specific detail to flatter his patron, King James</u>. What the Banquo descendant is carrying suggests that he is king of two countries as well as the ruler of a third region. <u>King James became king of both Scotland and England, and ruler of Wales. He also claimed to be a descendant of Banquo.</u>

### Student answer B

<u>Shakespeare's patron was King James I, who was also King of Scotland. James was descended from Banquo.</u>

Answer B will probably make you think, 'and your point is?' The contextual information given might be right, but it is not helpful. In fact, it is all context and no comment. By contrast, the contextual information in answer A adds to our understanding of the play by explaining the possible significance of a detail in the play that might otherwise be puzzling. A typical AQA exam-style question where context could be used might be:

### AQA exam-style questions

*[Starting with this extract,]* explore how far Shakespeare presents Malcolm as a model of good kingship in *Macbeth*.

'Malcolm as a model of good kingship' is a clear focus of the question. How far he is presented as a good model of kingship is partly a matter of *your thoughtful interpretation.* You *might* assess Malcolm's kingly qualities in the context of:

- the typical expectations of a king in Macbeth's time, Shakespeare's time, or even our own time

- what *you* think about monarchs or national leadership.

# REVIEW IT!

1  Which one of the following is the best definition of 'theme'?

  a  Something the play is about.

  b  Music at the start of the play.

  c  The order in which things happen in the play.

2  Give three other words that mean (or roughly mean) 'trust'.

3  Give three other words that mean (or roughly mean) 'power'.

4  Give three other words that mean (or roughly mean) 'evil'.

5  Give three other words that mean (or roughly mean) 'madness'.

6  In the play, which three characters are or become king of Scotland?

7  What does Lady Macbeth believe might stop Macbeth from achieving her ambition?

8  Why does Lady Macbeth tell Macbeth to 'look up clear'?

9  Why does Lady Macbeth wish that Macbeth was 'so much more the man'?

10  Why does Macduff not want Lady Macduff to hear about Duncan's murder?

11  Here are five themes: power, deception, madness, guilt, ambition.
    Which two of these themes are most relevant to the following quotation:

> **LADY MACBETH**
> You must leave this.
>
> **MACBETH**
> O, full of scorpions is my mind, dear wife!

12  Give three examples from Act 3 Scene 2 of a powerful character showing kindness or gratitude.

13  Explain what Macbeth means when he says:

> I am in blood
> Stepp'd in so far that, should I wade no more,
> Returning were as tedious as go o'er. (Act 3 Scene 4)

14  Give another example of a character realising it is pointless to regret what has already happened.

15  Read Lady Macbeth's speech in Act 1 Scene 5 that begins, 'Your face, my Thane…', up to '…serpent under it.' How are these words particularly effective at conveying the importance of appearances?

For the next five questions, choose an extract of the play which is no more than 15 lines long that is relevant to the theme identified. Write a paragraph to explain the relevance of that extract.

16  The theme of ambition.

17  The theme of guilt.

18  The theme of power.

19  The theme of deception.

20  The theme of evil and the supernatural.

# Language, structure and form

## Language

### The language of Shakespeare

When we talk about the language of a text, we mean how the writer *chooses* words to create effects. In other words, we are studying the writer's word *choices*. Shakespeare's language – although often brilliant – is sometimes unfamiliar for a modern audience.

### Language effects

Look at this famous line from *Macbeth*. Sleepwalking, Lady Macbeth is obsessively trying to erase the evidence of her guilt – Duncan's blood:

> Out, damned spot! Out, I say! (Act 5 Scene 1)

Shakespeare's simple choice of language expresses Lady Macbeth's state of mind very directly: she is desperate to lose the guilt which threatens her with being sent to hell ('damned'). The language is uncomplicated so as not to get in the way of a simple idea. On the other hand, Shakespeare's choices include some subtleties: the repetition of the imperative verb 'out' give the words a rhythm and a determination that show that Lady Macbeth is still trying to retain control. It is the *appropriateness* of Shakespeare's language choices that make them so impressive. Here is a student writing about the effects of Shakespeare's *precision* just a few lines later:

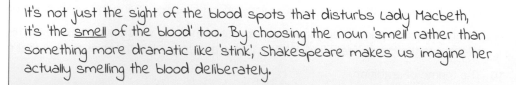
It's not just the sight of the blood spots that disturbs Lady Macbeth, it's 'the <u>smell</u> of the blood' too. By choosing the noun 'smell' rather than something more dramatic like 'stink', Shakespeare makes us imagine her actually smelling the blood deliberately.

### Imagery

Some patterns of imagery are developed in the play. Such patterns relate to darkness, illness, clothing and the supernatural.

For example, a contrast between light and dark is present in most of the play. Banquo calls the witches 'instruments of darkness' and night and darkness are welcomed by the Macbeths as a cover for their evil acts. Daylight represents 'the good things' before 'night's black agents' have their way (Act 3 Scene 2). By contrast, light (honesty and goodness) struggles to break through because 'dark night strangles' the day (Act 2 Scene 4): darkness defeats the light. Shakespeare often personifies night in this way, making the evil it represents active, stealthy and threatening. Lady Macbeth tries to fend off her 'dark' fears and guilt by having 'a light by her continually' (Act 5 Scene 1). When she dies, it is appropriate that Macbeth responds with, 'Out, out, brief candle!' (Act 5 Scene 5). This metaphor for life is effective not just because the play has taught us how vulnerable light (goodness and truth) is, but also because of the connotations of 'candle': it wavers, is easily blown out, and its light does not travel far. It perfectly captures the vulnerability and insignificance of human lives. It is an original and striking image, and striking *because* of its originality.

Look at how Macbeth continues to personify life:

> It is a tale
> Told by an idiot, full of sound and fury,
> Signifying nothing.

## Proverbial speech

Another striking aspect of Shakespeare's language in *Macbeth* is his use of proverbial speech. A proverb is a well-known saying that people use to make sense of situations: for example, 'A drowning man will clutch at a straw' (meaning, when you are desperate, you will cling to anything). Because a proverb is a metaphor, it can be symbolically applied to many situations and it sounds wise. Here is one example of proverbial speech in *Macbeth*:

> Things bad begun make strong themselves by ill. (Act 3 Scene 2)

Here Macbeth is making the *general* observation that evil acts can only be protected and strengthened by more evil acts.

Here are two more examples of proverbial speech in *Macbeth*:

> Words to the heat of deeds too cold breath gives. (Macbeth, Act 2 Scene 1)
> The night is long that never finds the day. (Malcolm, Act 4 Scene 3)

Consider:
- Do I like this description of life?
- Is it effective?
- Do I *dis*like the description in any way? If so, why?

Find two other examples of proverbial speech in the play.

Explain the meaning of each example *as it is used in the play.*

Don't be put off by Shakespeare's language – you can get by without understanding every word. The effort to understand it is worth it!

## Writing about Shakespeare's language in Macbeth

Some examples of Shakespeare's language are worth exploring in depth. Take Macbeth's realisation that Malcolm would need to die for Macbeth to become king:

> Stars, hide your fires;/Let not light see my black and deep desires. (Act 1 Scene 4)

Now read one student's analysis of these words. Notice the way the student:

- refers to details in the text

- examines the *effect* and significance of the *way* Macbeth speaks.

> The way that Macbeth speaks here shows he has quickly moved from his stunned ('rapt') reaction to the witches' predictions to something much more controlled and deliberate. He speaks (or thinks) directly to the stars (fate) and immediately pauses before confidently telling them to work for him. The imperative verb 'hide' shows his commanding, decisive frame of mind. The words he chooses make it quite clear that he has gone over to the dark, evil side of his persona, while he associates light with the goodness and trustworthiness he is abandoning. His evil decisiveness is further stressed by the neat rhymes, 'desires'/'fires'. This decisiveness is fully evident *before* he has spoken to Lady Macbeth.

## Structure

*Macbeth* is organised into five acts that divide the plot into stages. Act 1 could be labelled 'deciding to kill Duncan'.

### The three unities theory

Shakespeare would have been aware of the traditional theory that plays should stick to the 'three unities' of place, time and action. According to this theory the action of the play should:

- have one, chronological plot

- happen in one place

- happen in one short time frame.

*Macbeth* pays some respect to the three unities: the plot is straightforward; its action happens in weeks or months rather than years, and mostly in or around Macbeth's castle. Macbeth himself develops through clear stages that *could* be identified as:

| Stage | Explanation |
|---|---|
| Heroic self-sacrifice | Macbeth is a national war hero. He puts king and country above his own safety. |
| Temptation | The witches and Lady Macbeth influence him. |
| The fall into evil | He accepts the temptation and supresses his conscience. |
| The pursuit of absolute power | He commits any evil necessary to protect the position he has won by force. |
| Inevitable downfall/ personal suffering | We know he is heading for defeat because we don't trust the witches. Macbeth suffers insomnia, madness and bereavement. |
| Punishment by death. | Macduff serves justice on Macbeth by killing him. |

**DO IT!**

What do *you* consider to be the key things Shakespeare would want us to learn from the play?

Write down your ideas.

Try to define the things we are meant to learn as precisely as possible.

## Structure and meaning

The play's structure, therefore, is **didactic** – we learn about important limits that should be placed on 'ambition' by accompanying Macbeth through his rise and fall.

**STRETCHIT!**

How do you think we should feel about the Macbeths during Act 5?

How does the way we feel about the Macbeths in Act 5 affect what we learn from the play?

### Tragedy

*Macbeth* is one of Shakespeare's most famous tragedies. A traditional **tragedy** shows us a person of high status falling from triumph, through suffering, to disaster and destruction. Personal weaknesses contribute to the fall of the tragic hero. At the start of the play Macbeth is hailed as a hero, but by the end he is humiliated, hated and dead. Whether or not he is a tragic hero depends on whether you think he is evil to his core, or is 'turned' evil.

# Form

Shakespeare wrote in three different forms:

- prose
- **blank verse**
- rhyming verse.

## Prose

Nearly all of *Macbeth* is written in poetry ('verse'), with just a few brief sections in prose. Prose can give **dialogue** a more down-to-earth feel than poetry can. For example, at the beginning of the 'banquet scene' (Act 3 Scene 4) when Macbeth is being informal and putting his guests at their ease, Shakespeare writes Macbeth's lines in prose. The 'sleepwalking' scene (Act 5 Scene 1) is also written in prose. Perhaps Shakespeare decided prose better suited the looseness of Lady Macbeth's sleep-talking.

## Blank verse and iambic pentameter

Much of the threatening mood of *Macbeth* is created by its powerful poetry. Except for the witches' entrancing speeches, the poetry is based around iambic pentameter: each line has exactly – or nearly – ten syllables and a repeated pattern of beats, starting with an unstressed syllable and then alternating between stressed and unstressed. Iambic pentameter gives the noble characters – such as Ross and Malcolm – a dignified authority. When used by the Macbeths, iambic pentameter showcases the cruel, sinister content of their speeches. Macbeth's words below are underlined to show the iambic patterning:

> "
> The <u>cry</u> is <u>still</u>, "They <u>come</u>." Our <u>castle's</u> <u>strength</u>
> Will <u>laugh</u> a <u>siege</u> to <u>scorn</u>. Here <u>let</u> them <u>lie</u>
> Till <u>famine</u> <u>and</u> the <u>ague</u> <u>eat</u> them <u>up</u>.
> "

The first and second lines are perfect iambic pentameters. The second stress in line 3 is less easy to place.

## Rhyme

Sometimes Shakespeare ends lines with a rhyme. This has a number of effects. It can:

- give the line – and therefore an idea contained in it – special emphasis
- give a neat, firm conclusion to a scene or a speech
- make a line more memorable so that audiences recall it in later scenes where its key idea can gain greater significance.

Rhyme, coupled with iambic rhythm, is particularly effective at emphasising ideas and moods. Here is an example:

## Extract 1

**MACBETH**
I will not be afraid of death and bane,
Till Birnam Forest come to Dunsinane.

**DOCTOR**
Were I from Dunsinane away and clear,
Profit again should hardly draw me here.
*Exeunt*

> The 'bane'/'ane' rhyme strengthens the rhythm of the lines, giving heavy emphasis to Macbeth's tone of determination.

> By repeating the form of Macbeth's words – an iambic rhyming couplet, the Doctor's words mock Macbeth's idea about the safety of Dunsinane. The Doctor states the exact opposite: he'd escape forever if he could.

### NAILIT!

To do well in your AQA exam, you need to develop and defend your own view of Macbeth:

- To what extent is he a *victim* of outside influences and of his own weaknesses?
- What are his weaknesses?
- Can we feel any sympathy for him?

## REVIEW IT!

1 What does 'thou' mean?

2 What does 'thy' mean?

3 What does 'hast' mean?

4 What does 'dost' mean?

5 When we talk about 'language' we are not talking about whether the play is written in English or another language, so what do we mean?

6 Name two good reasons for not being put off by Shakespeare's language.

7 What is a simile?

8 What is a metaphor?

9 What is personification?

10 What is prose?

11 What is 'blank verse'?

12 What is the term for a line of poetry with ten syllables that alternate between unstressed and stressed?

13 What is the metaphor in these two lines?

> They have tied me to the stake; I cannot fly,/ But bear-like I must fight the course.'
> (Macbeth, Act 5 Scene 7)

14 Comment on the effect of this metaphor.

15 Why do you think the word 'brandish'd' has an apostrophe instead of an 'e'?

16 How do the highlighted words below show Malcolm's strength of leadership?

> Be this the whetstone of your sword. Let grief/Convert to anger; (Act 4 Scene 3)

17 Comment on the effect of the word 'filling' in Macbeth's report that Duncan's sons have fled and are 'filling their hearers/With strange invention.' (Act 3 Scene 1)

18 Explain what Macbeth means when he complains that:

> Upon my head they *[the witches]* plac'd a fruitless crown
> And put a barren sceptre in my gripe (Act 3 Scene 1)

19 Find a place in the play where lines suddenly rhyme. Why do you think Shakespeare switched to rhyme? What do you think is the effect of the switch to rhyme?

20 Explain how the play's structure helps to keep the interest of the audience. Are there any places where the audience's attention might start to wander? If so, why?

# Doing well in your AQA exam

## Understanding the question

**NAILIT!**

In your AQA exam, the extract will come before the question, but it is a good idea to **read the question before you read the extract**. That way you will read the extract with the question focus in mind.

Make sure you understand the exam question so that you do not include irrelevant material in your answer.

The question below has been annotated by a student so that they are clear about what it is asking for.

The extract

Sh.'s methods

How and why Sh. creates their relationship – how should we react to them?

Starting with this conversation, explore how Shakespeare presents the relationship between Macbeth and Banquo in *Macbeth*.

Not the two separately – their relationship.

Write about:

- how Shakespeare presents the relationship between Macbeth and Banquo in this extract

- how Shakespeare presents the relationship between Macbeth and Banquo in the play as a whole.

How he makes us feel about their relationship – what is he suggesting? Might we react in ways that Shakespeare could not predict?

This student has studied the question carefully and realised that:

- the focus is on the relationship between Macbeth and Banquo

- 'present' means not just describing that relationship but also identifying Shakespeare's intentions

- a modern audience might react differently from how Shakespeare might have intended.

'Pinning the question down' like this – making sure it is fully understood – has allowed the student to then pick out of the extract some useful evidence to support the answer.

**DOIT!**

Choose another AQA exam-style question from earlier in this guide. Annotate the question and the extract.

# Planning your answer

Once you have fully understood the question, planning an answer will be quite straightforward. Your brief plan should set out:

- your key, *relevant* ideas
- the content of each of four or five main paragraphs
- the order of the paragraphs.

Here is the same student's plan for their answer to the exam question on page 84:

**NAILIT!**

High-level answers should have four or five well-planned paragraphs (plus a brief introduction and conclusion).

| Paragraph | Content | | Timing plan |
|---|---|---|---|
| 1 | Intro - use the question preparation to establish focus of answer | | 9.40 |
| 2 | Explore extract - evidence of close relationship | | 9.43 |
| 3 | Hints of division - pay attention to language subtleties | Refer back to extract and question focus sometimes. Question their 'relationship' and what Sh. might be implying. | 9.58 |
| 4 | How their relationship becomes false, over respectful, hiding mutual distrust | | 10.06 |
| 5 | How Sh. uses the relationship to convey contrasts in their views: they represent different values, so relationship underpins Sh.'s meaning. (How might King James have responded to the two characters?) | | 10.14 |
| 6 | Conclusion - brief return to question/would a modern audience trust Banquo? | | 10.22 |

## Sticking to the plan

Note how this student has even jotted down time points when they should move on to the next section of their answer. That way they make sure they do not get stuck on one point and fail to cover the question focus in enough breadth.

## Planning to meet the mark scheme

The plan above suggests that the student has thought carefully about the focus of the question, that they are familiar with the mark scheme for their AQA Shakespeare question and are planning to cover its requirements. (See the summary mark scheme on page 86.)

**DOIT!**

Go back to the exam question which you chose and annotated for the Do it! on page 84. Develop a brief plan for it as above.

| Assessment objective | What the plan promises |
|---|---|
| **AO1 understand and respond** | Understanding of a number of ideas relevant to the main question focus - close relationship as well as hints of division.<br><br>Some personal interpretations to be included - suggested by consideration of how the relationship conveys meanings in the play. |
| **AO2 language, form and structure** | Exploring extract will ensure close engagement with Shakespeare's language and poetic form. Annotations already point to this. |
| **AO3 context** | Consideration of:<br>• how modern audience might view Banquo in the relationship.<br>• how King James might have responded |

# What your AQA examiner is looking for

Your AQA examiner will mark your answer according to a mark scheme based on four assessment objectives (AOs). The AOs focus on specific knowledge, understanding and skills. AO4 – which is about vocabulary, sentence structures, spelling and punctuation – is worth four marks. Together, the other AOs are worth 30 marks, so it is important to understand what the examiner is looking out for.

## Mark scheme

Your AQA examiner will mark your answers in 'bands'. These bands roughly equate as follows:

- band 6 approx. grades 8 and 9
- band 5 approx. grades 6 and 7
- band 4 approx. grades 5 and 6
- band 3 approx. grades 3 and 4
- band 2 approx. grades 1 and 2.

Most importantly, the improvement descriptors in the table below will help you understand how to improve your answers and, therefore, gain more marks. The maximum number of marks for each AO is shown.

| Assessment objective (AO) | | Improvement descriptors | | | | |
|---|---|---|---|---|---|---|
| | | Band 2<br>Your answer… | Band 3<br>Your answer… | Band 4<br>Your answer… | Band 5<br>Your answer… | Band 6<br>Your answer… |
| AO1<br>12 marks | Read, understand and respond | is relevant and backs up ideas with references to the play. | sometimes explains the play in relation to the question. | clearly explains the play in relation to the question. | thoughtfully explains the play in relation to the question. | critically explores the play in relation to the question. |
| | Use evidence | makes some comments about these references. | refers to details in the play to back up points. | carefully chooses close references to the play to back up points. | thoughtfully builds appropriate references into points. | chooses precise details from the play to make points convincing. |
| AO2<br>12 marks | Language, form and structure | mentions some of Shakespeare's methods. | comments on some of Shakespeare's methods and their effects. | clearly explains Shakespeare's key methods and their effects. | thoughtfully explores Shakespeare's methods and their effects. | analyses Shakespeare's methods and how these influence the reader and/or audience. |
| | Subject terminology | uses some subject terminology. | uses some relevant terminology. | helpfully uses varied, relevant terminology. | makes thoughtful use of relevant terminology. | chooses subject terminology to make points precise and convincing. |
| AO3<br>6 marks | Contexts | makes some simple inferences about contexts. | infers Shakespeare's point of view and the significance of contexts. | shows a clear appreciation of Shakespeare's point of view and the significance of contexts. | explores Shakespeare's point of view and the significance of relevant contexts. | makes perceptive and revealing links between the play and relevant contexts. |

## AO1 Read, understand and respond/Use evidence

Make sure you read and answer the question carefully and thoughtfully. Your examiner will be looking out for evidence that you have answered the actual question on the paper. The more thoughtful and relevant your answer the better. Do not make the mistake of going into your exam with an answer in mind: you must concentrate on the aspect or theme that the question focuses on. Knowing the play well will give you the confidence to do that.

'Use evidence' means supporting your ideas with references to the playscript. They can be indirect references – brief mentions of an event or what a character says or does – or direct references – quotations. Choose and use evidence carefully so that it clearly supports a point you are making. Quotations should be as short as possible, and the very best ones are often neatly built into your own writing.

## AO2 Language, form and structure/Subject terminology

The characters in *Macbeth* are not real people; they have been *created* by Shakespeare to entertain and influence the audience. Good answers will explore how Shakespeare chooses language to create characters and situations, and to have effects on the audience.

**Subject terminology** is about choosing your words carefully, using the right words and avoiding vague expressions. It is also about using terminology *helpfully*. For example, here are two different uses of subject terminology, the first much more useful than the second:

> **Student answer A**
> Describing the guards as 'steep'd in the colours of their trade' is shockingly graphic. The 'trade' euphemism shocks us by making murder sound like an everyday job. Macbeth is using sarcasm to express his outrage.

> **Student answer B**
> 'Trade' is a good euphemism for murder.

## AO3 Contexts

Notice the emphasis on '*relevant* contexts' higher up the mark criteria. The best answers will include contextual information that is directly relevant to the *question*, not just the play. (See answer A on page 76 for a good example.) Consider how might:

- the society Shakespeare lived in have influenced his ideas and attitudes?
- the society *you* live in influence how *you* respond to ideas and attitudes in the play?
- knowledge of the whole play enrich your understanding of the extract?

## AO4 Vocabulary, sentence structures, spelling and punctuation

Check your spelling and punctuation. Use a range of vocabulary and sentence structures for clarity, purpose and effect.

**NAILIT!**

To boost your marks, when answering questions do the following:

- Know the play well. Read it and study it.
- Don't go into your exam with ready-prepared answers.
- Read the question and make sure you answer it thoughtfully.
- Choose details from the play that will support your points.
- Don't treat the play and its characters as though they are real. Instead ask why Shakespeare has chosen to create a particular dialogue or event. What effect is he trying to achieve?

# Writing your answer

## Getting started

Here are the openings of two students' answers to the question on page 84 about how Shakespeare presents the relationship between Macbeth and Banquo in *Macbeth*.

### Student answer A

Although Banquo and Macbeth led their army and – according to the wounded Captain – fought alongside each other, their relationship weakens surprisingly quickly, and by Act 2 they are already becoming distanced from each other. I am going to argue that Shakespeare wants us to notice the cracks in their relationship right from the beginning, and that he presents the two characters as opposites, not true partners.

### Student answer B

I am going to write about the relationship between Macbeth and Banquo and how it changes. They are partners in commanding the army and are friends, but also have a lot of different views. Macbeth is out for what he can get but Banquo wants to be loyal to the king and only do the right thing. Those are the sorts of things I'm going to write about in my answer about Macbeth in answer to the exam question about...

**DOIT!**

Student A's is the better introduction. Explain why using the success criteria on page 86.

## The extract

You do not need to write about the extract and *then* about the rest of the play. You *can* compare the extract with other parts of the play throughout your answer. However, a safe approach – just to make sure you give the extract enough attention – is to begin with the extract and then make connections with other parts of the play in the following paragraphs. This is the approach suggested in the plan you have already looked at.

Here is part of that student's third paragraph. Note how they closely examine relevant details of Shakespeare's language choices. An examiner has made some comments in the margin.

The way they speak to each other confirms their relationship as 'partners', but also hints at some underlying divisions. Their 'partnership' is implied by the way they ask each other questions to jointly make sense of their experience. Their dialogue explores the disappearance of the witches in a poetic way as though simple words are inadequate, and Macbeth's poetic description of the witches' disappearance - 'Melted as breath into the wind' - builds on Banquo's struggle to define the insubstantiality of the witches' 'bubbles'. By adopting the style of Banquo's description, Macbeth respects it and develops it. Yet despite this unity suggested by the way they converse, there are hints that they do not entirely trust each other. For example...

Good topic sentence setting out a clear point that is referenced to wording in the exam question.

Precise and useful terminology.

Effect of words is identified.

Direct evidence used well – built neatly into student's own words.

# Paragraph topics

Each of your paragraphs should deal with a subtopic of the main focus of the question. The plan you have already looked at suggests that the next three paragraph topics will be: hints of division, then distrust, then what they represent. This last paragraph will help the student to directly consider the 'how Shakespeare presents' aspect of the question: they will have to consider what Shakespeare is trying to suggest via the contrast between the two characters.

Below you will see how – in their 'what they represent' paragraph – the same student makes references back to both the extract and the question so as to stay sharply relevant. The references are underlined to point them out.

> The relationship between Macbeth and Banquo stretches as they go in different directions, offering the audience alternative models of moral choices. As they part for the last time, Macbeth wishes Banquo a safe journey, and so their relationship is still polite and friendly, and Macbeth still treats Banquo as a partner: he reminds Banquo that on the following day, 'we shall have cause of state/Craving us jointly.' However, the audience knows that Macbeth is arranging Banquo's murder, and Banquo suspects Macbeth of having 'played'st most foully' to become king. Compared with the easy conversation they enjoyed in the extract, their dialogue is now restrained and falsely respectful. Shakespeare presents a clear choice for the audience: they can take the side of either evil and treachery represented by Macbeth, or loyalty and honesty represented by Banquo.

Using evidence:

This student makes their points using precise terminology, direct evidence in the form of quotations, as well as indirect evidence when referring to another part of the text. Both forms of evidence are valid, but do quote from the extract at least – if only to show you can handle quotations.

# Ending your answer

If you write a conclusion, make it useful: don't simply repeat what you have already said. The answer we have been looking at ends by summarising the student's personal response:

> On balance I think that Shakespeare presents Banquo and Macbeth as 'partners' only through circumstance. Really they are presented as moral opposites for us to choose between. The choice should be easy, but why does Shakespeare make Banquo so dull, and Macbeth so interesting?!

In fact, this conclusion adds little to the student's answer. It merely restates their overall point: Banquo and Macbeth are presented as opposites. The last sentence raises a fascinating question, but it would have been better placed in an earlier paragraph where it could have been explored.

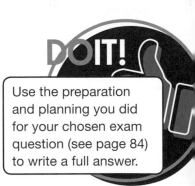

Use the preparation and planning you did for your chosen exam question (see page 84) to write a full answer.

## STRETCHIT!

Develop a range of evaluative vocabulary to enable you to pinpoint Shakespeare's intention. Use words like: 'condemns', 'criticises', 'exposes', 'ridicules', 'subverts', 'questions'.

## Going for the top grades

Of course, you will always try to write the best answer possible, but if you are aiming for the top grades then it is vital to be clear about what examiners will be looking out for. The best answers will:

| | |
|---|---|
| • develop a conceptual response to the exam question | **AO1** |
| • show insight into the play and the question focus by developing a clear argument | |
| • explore meaning in the play in relation to the focus of the question | |
| • choose and use evidence precisely and wisely | |
| • analyse Shakespeare's methods and their effect on the reader | **AO2** |
| • use relevant, helpful subject terminology | |
| • explore aspects of context that are relevant to the play and the question. | **AO3** |

### Conceptual response

A conceptual response means establishing a particular 'angle' on the question focus, and using that angle as a reference point for the whole answer. For example, take the answer you have been looking at about the relationship between Macbeth and Banquo. The student's final thought – about why Shakespeare makes Banquo dull and Macbeth interesting – could have made a fascinating conceptual focus for their whole answer.

The best answers will be RIPE with ideas and engagement:

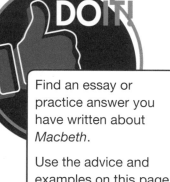

| R | • Relevant | Stay strictly relevant to the question. |
|---|---|---|
| I | • Insightful | Develop relevant insights into the play, its characters, themes and dramatic techniques. |
| P | • Precise | Choose and use evidence precisely so that it strengthens your points. |
| E | • Exploratory | Explore relevant aspects of the play, looking at it from more than one angle. |

Below is part of a student's answer to the question: how does Shakespeare present leadership in *Macbeth*? The student is developing the challenging idea that Shakespeare presents some aspects of Macbeth's actions in a positive light. Next to the answer are some comments by an examiner.

Even Macbeth might have represented some positive aspects of leadership for King James I. Macbeth might have become a king-killing villain, but at the start of the play he is clearly a king-saving hero, admired by Duncan, inspiring his 'wonders and his praises.' Macbeth's instinct is to sacrifice his own safety ('disdaining fortune') for the sake of the safety of his king and country. Even when he has agreed to murder Duncan he is reluctant to go ahead because of his instinctive loyalty to his king as Duncan's subject, Macbeth is 'strong...against the deed.' Perhaps what really motivates Macbeth to kill Duncan is that Duncan's weak leadership has endangered Scotland's independence...

Original insight related to context.

Complexities of Macbeth's mindset introduced here.

Precise evidence neatly integrated into argument.

Tentatively introduced insight/ hypothesis.

Good return to question focus to maintain relevance.

# REVIEW IT!

1  What should you do before you read the extract from the play?
2  Why should you do that before reading the extract?
3  How long should you spend on understanding the question and planning your answer?
4  What three things should be covered in your plan?

5  Why is it helpful to build timings into your plan?
6  How many paragraphs is a good number to plan for?
7  Why is it useful to know the mark scheme?
8  Should you write an introduction and a conclusion?
9  Do you have to write about the extract before writing about the rest of the play?
10  What should each paragraph of your answer be about?
11  Must you quote from the extract?
12  What is meant by 'evidence'?
13  What should be the focus of your revision in the final month?
14  It is vital that your answer is relevant. Relevant to what?
15  What four ideas should be kept in mind when trying to write a top grade answer?
16  Why is this a bad conclusion to an answer?

> So that is what I think - Macbeth only has himself to blame.
> I think I've made it clear why.

17  Why is this a slightly better conclusion?

> So, in the end it probably depends on your view of Macbeth. You could admire his bravery and refusal to accept defeat, or you might condemn him for his immorality and for his foolish inability to resist temptation.

18  Here is an exam question. Annotate the question to help you understand it fully.

*[Starting with this speech,]* explore how Shakespeare presents evil and the supernatural in *Macbeth*

19  Write a plan for an answer to the question above.
20  Write one main paragraph that you have planned for.

On these pages you will find two practice questions for *Macbeth*. Self-assessment guidance is provided on the app/online. In the exam you will only get one question: you will not have a choice of questions.

## PRACTICE QUESTION 1

Read the following extract from Act 3 Scene 4 of *Macbeth* and then answer the question that follows.

At this point in the play, the Macbeths' guests are alarmed by Macbeth's erratic behaviour after seeing Banquo's ghost.

> **LADY MACBETH**
> Sit, worthy friends; my lord is often thus,
> And hath been from his youth. Pray you, keep seat.
> The fit is momentary; upon a thought
> He will again be well. If much you note him,
> 5 You shall offend him and extend his passion.
> Feed, and regard him not – Are you a man?
>
> **MACBETH**
> Ay, and a bold one, that dare look on that
> Which might appal the devil.
>
> **LADY MACBETH**
> O proper stuff!
> 10 This is the very painting of your fear;
> This is the air-drawn dagger which you said
> Led you to Duncan. O, these flaws and starts,
> Impostors to true fear, would well become
> A woman's story at a winter's fire,
> 15 Authorized by her grandam. Shame itself!
> Why do you make such faces? When all's done,
> You look but on a stool.

Starting with this moment in the play, explore how far Shakespeare presents Lady Macbeth as a loyal and supportive partner to Macbeth in *Macbeth*.

Write about:

- how Shakespeare presents Lady Macbeth at this moment in the play

- how Shakespeare presents Lady Macbeth in the play as a whole.

[30 marks]
AO4 [4 marks]

## PRACTICE QUESTION 2

Read the following extract from Act 1 Scene 1 of *Macbeth* and then answer the question that follows.

This is the opening of the play. The witches are planning to meet Macbeth on his way back from the battle.

*A deserted place. Thunder and lightning.*
*Enter THREE WITCHES*

**FIRST WITCH**
When shall we three meet again?
In thunder, lightning, or in rain?

**SECOND WITCH**
When the hurlyburly's done,
When the battle's lost and won.

**THIRD WITCH**
5  That will be ere the set of sun.

**FIRST WITCH**
Where the place?

**SECOND WITCH**
Upon the heath.

**THIRD WITCH**
There to meet with Macbeth.

**FIRST WITCH**
I come, Graymalkin!

**SECOND WITCH**
10  Paddock calls.

**THIRD WITCH**
Anon!

**ALL**
Fair is foul, and foul is fair.
Hover through the fog and filthy air.                    [*Exeunt*]

Starting with this conversation, explore how Shakespeare presents evil and the supernatural in *Macbeth.*

Write about:

- how Shakespeare presents evil and the supernatural in this conversation

- how Shakespeare presents evil and the supernatural in the play as a whole.

**[30 marks]**
**AO4 [4 marks]**

# Glossary

**adjective** A word that describes a noun (for example: *dreadful* note; *restless* ecstasy).

**alliteration** Words starting with the same sound and placed near each other for effect (for example: *cabin'd, cribb'd, confin'd*).

**blank verse** Poetry that does not rhyme.

**character** A person in a play or story: a person created by the writer (for example: Macbeth, Lady Macbeth or Banquo).

**connotation** An implied meaning. See **implicit.**

**context** The circumstances in which a play was written or is watched. These could include normal beliefs at the turn of the 17th century, or the typical attitudes of a 21st-century audience.

**didactic** Designed to teach a particular lesson.

**dialogue** The words that characters say in plays or in fiction. In fiction, these words are usually shown with speech marks ("…").

**dramatic irony** When the audience knows more than a character (for example, at the beginning of Act 1 Scene 6 when Duncan and Banquo feel safe and relaxed but the audience knows that Duncan is far from safe).

**dramatist** Playwright: the author of a play.

**effect** The impact that a writer's words have on a reader: the mood, feeling or reaction the words create in the reader/viewer.

**euphemism** A softened word or phrase used instead of a harsh, direct one (for example: *passed on* instead of *died*).

**explicit** Explicit information is clearly stated; it's on the surface of a text and should be obvious.

**enjambement** When a line of poetry does not end with punctuation but instead its sense runs straight into the next line.

**hyperbole** Exaggerated statements or claims not meant to be taken literally. Used for rhetorical effect.

**imperative verb** A 'command' word; verbs used to give instructions (for example: *sit, think, understand*).

**imagery** The 'pictures' an author puts into the reader's mind. Similes and metaphors are common types of imagery. Macbeth is full of imagery linked to clothes, darkness, night.

**implicit (imply)** Implicit information is only suggested (or implied), it is not stated directed; we have to infer to understand it. The opposite of explicit. See **explicit.**

**interpret** Use clues to work out meanings or the feelings or motives of a character.

**iambic pentameter** A line of poetry that consists of five iambic feet (or 'iambs') so that the line follows an unstressed/stressed pattern (for example: 'That *dark*ness *does* the *face* of *earth* en*tomb*.').

**language** The words and the style that a writer *chooses* in order to have an effect on a reader.

**metaphor** Comparing two things by referring to them as though they are the same thing (for example, Macbeth says his mind is *'full of scorpions'*. It is not *literally* full of scorpions.).

**monosyllable** A word with just one syllable (for example: *Ross, thane, my*).

**personify/personification** To give an abstract concept such as night a character. For example, in *Macbeth* the night is described as having hands.

**phrase** A group of words within a sentence.

**playscript** The words written by the playwright for the actors to perform.

**playwright** The author of a play.

**plot** The story of the play: the sequence of the events and how they link together.

**prose** Writing that is not poetry.

**proverb** A wise saying.

**rhetorical question** A question that does not need an answer. Normally used for persuasive purposes.

**rhyme** Words chosen by a poet because they have the same sound (for example: *he/flea; stable/label; laughter/after*).

**rhyming couplet** Two consecutive lines that rhyme.

**rhythm** The beat in poetry or music.

**simile** Describing something by comparing it with something else. For example: Macbeth will seem '*as pure as snow*'; the Captain describes Macbeth as '*like valour's minion*'.

**structure** How a text is organised and held together: all those things that shape a text and make it coherent. For example, Macbeth is arranged into five acts; it follows the sequence of a traditional 'tragedy'; it has repeated patterns of imagery of the supernatural, for example.

**subject terminology** The technical words that are used in a particular subject. All the words in this glossary are subject terminology for English literature.

**tone** The mood of a text, or the attitude of the author or narrator towards the topic. For example, tones can be mocking, affectionate, polite, authoritative.

**tragedy** A form of drama in which a hero's life ends in disaster, normally through a combination of bad luck, fate and their own personal weaknesses.

**verse** Poetry that has a regular form in terms of rhythm and/or rhyme.

# SCHOLASTIC

# AQA ENGLISH STUDY GUIDES

## THE BEST WAY TO GET TO KNOW YOUR ENGLISH LITERATURE SET TEXTS

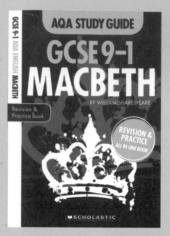

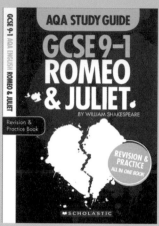

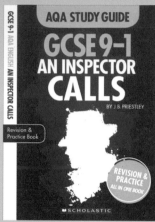

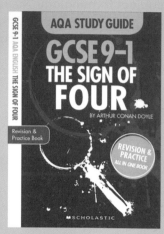

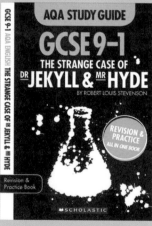

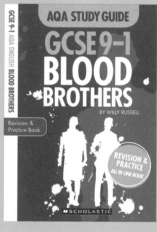

# DISCOVER YOUR NEXT CLASSIC READ

Unforgettable stories by the best authors